Sneaker Resale & Retail in the New Normal
By Christopher D. Burns, MFA

CB Publishing
2020

Copyright © 2020 by Christopher D. Burns, MFA

ISBN Amazon: 9798639558290

ISBN Lulu: 978716912160

All rights reserved. This paper or any portion thereof may not be reproduced or used in any manner whatsoever without the express written permission of the publisher except for the use of brief quotations in a book review or scholarly journal.

CB Publishing

www.cbpublish.com

www.arch-usa.com

Please contact Christopher D. Burns at cdburns@cbpublish.com or visit www.arch-usa.com

Ordering Information:

Special discounts are available on quantity purchases by corporations, associations, educators, and others. For details, contact the publisher at the above listed address.

U.S. trade bookstores and wholesalers: Please contact Christopher D. Burns at cdburns@cbpublish.com or visit www.arch-usa.com

Books by Christopher D. Burns, MFA

One Hour to Wealth: Your Great Idea is Valuable; Get Up & Write It Down

The 30 Day Project: How Daily Dedication Can Lead to Something Amazing

F- -k Speeches & Inspiration: Where Do I Get the Money to Start?

Nike's Consumer Direct Offense, Amazon & StockX: The Disruption of Sneaker Retail

Dedication

This book was going to be about how I made over a million dollars on StockX in 18 months. I decided to adjust the book as COVID-19 has completely reshaped the landscape for the sneaker industry in ways that we won't understand for years.

The book is dedicated to my friends, peers and everyone who has been impacted by the virus and quarantine. There aren't any clichés that can uplift when people are struggling. I won't write any platitudes or motivational words in this dedication. I only hope that we all find our way back to some sense of normal.

Table of Contents

Foreword . . . . . . pg. 11

Ch. 1 Should StockX Be Regulated? . . pg. 15

Ch. 2 Why Retailers Needed the adidas MakerLab Limited-Edition Campus 80s x StockX IPO to be Flawed . . pg. 27

Ch. 3 10 Reasons the 'adidas Campus 80s x StockX IPO' Was the Most Important Drop of the Year . . . pg. 35

Ch. 4 Why the Hack of StockX Didn't Hurt? . pg. 45

Ch. 5 10 Reasons the RealReal IPO and StockX's Unicorn Status Happened . . . . . . pg. 51

Ch. 6 StockX Buying Ad Time During the WNBA Season is More Important Than it Looks . . . pg. 59

Ch. 7 Nike's Supply Chain as Disruptor . . pg. 65

Ch. 8 The Democratization of Sneaker Resale . pg. 71

Ch. 9 Reintroduction. . . . pg. 85

Ch. 10 Remember, Sneaker Culture is Mainstream . pg. 93

Ch. 11 The Time is Now for Private Label and Startups   pg. 105

Ch. 12 Parents and Professionals = Forrest and Bubba pg. 115

Ch. 13 The Cash Customer is Finally Digital . pg. 127

Ch. 14 Opportunities and a Clean Slate . pg. 139

Ch. 15 Sustainability and Sharing as Opportunity . pg. 147

Ch. 16 Limited Opportunities Isn't a Bad Thing . pg. 155

Ch. 17 Addendum . . . . . pg. 165

Foreword

Typically a foreword is written by someone else as an explanation of what the reader will be diving into. There really isn't anyone who can be asked to explain what I'm about to jump into here. There are people, but they probably aren't willing to talk about what they do as openly and with the same amount of detail.

I wanted this book to initially address why I could work in the grey area of the sneaker industry and generate as much money as a store that holds accounts with all of the various sneaker brands and has a staff of employees, when I work by myself for the most part. I made a million dollars on StockX in less than eighteen months; 1.5 Million in two years. In my best year on Amazon I made half a million and from 2011 to 2016 I made a total of just over 2 Million dollars.

I shouldn't be able to do this. This book was going to be an eye opener about the shortcomings of retail, but with COVID-19 I have found that it isn't important to dig in and write what's wrong without offering a deeper understanding.

What I am doing here first is expanding discussions I created on arch-usa.com about StockX. What you will find is that I considered StockX to be a fragile platform that has evolved and built itself into an elegant solution as a digital warehouse and distribution option. They haven't begun to utilize it as much as they could; although at the time that I was editing this book they had launched another IPO with New Balance.

The idea of it being fragile is important; because if retail and brands were doing the things they are supposed to be doing, StockX would exist solely as a resale platform for items that are no longer in inventory at retail. Right now StockX caters to every demographic; when originally it was a site built around limited release and hard to find sneakers. The information that is the most important is that the site now reaches a broad spectrum of consumers with the same items that can be found in retail stores across the country.

As I wrote this book I questioned if building an analysis on a 3rd party middleman site like StockX is enough to make sense of the current operation of retail. I realized that StockX, and other businesses like it, are perfect for analyzing the changing retail landscape. Retail stores that carry other brands, or retailers who set out to carry other brands, are doing so in one of the most difficult moments in retail history.

In a world where brands can't reach every customer and they work with retail brick and mortar stores to get their products to those they don't have access to, retailers have to account for the reality that as they help build brands by carrying them, those same brands will expand and eventually become competitors and not just vendors. Direct-to Consumer is an amazing thing for a company, but the growth of DTC and the rise of third party websites make for a compelling retail discussion.

I hope what I'm attempting here works. It was much easier when I thought I'd only be talking about how I made over a million dollars using StockX. That book was going to be a fun analysis of reselling sneakers. COVID-19 has changed everything. My peers, friends, managers, district managers, buyers, and employees at retail chains are faced with the loss of jobs and the closure of stores. Peers who work for brands have been furloughed and laid off.

My work as a writer in the sneaker industry should be my primary job, but it's not. I work in the grey area because the money there is readily available. Both brands and retailers are failing to acknowledge the issues in the industry. The conversations in the sneaker industry happen in boardrooms between people who are insiders. Fixing the sneaker industry doesn't happen inside of an echo chamber of sameness with the old guard leading the discussion. The dialogue has to expand into the grey, cloudy waters where a subculture has become a multi-billion dollar industry built around tech functioning as the middleman.

Chapter

1

Should StockX Be Regulated?

The original name of this section was going to be, "Should StockX Implement a SRP Policy for the First Week of Release?" The discussion originated in a post on my website addressing the new Kyrie 6. The Kyrie 6 officially launched on 11/22/2019. The shoe was discussed on blogs and sneaker sites as a modernized version of the Air Yeezy 2. In sneaker culture the *Nike* Yeezy shoes are considered "grails" or highly coveted sneakers that could fetch a lot of money in the secondary marketplace. I state this to set the premise for this chapter. The Kyrie 6 was supposed to be a transitional shoe for Nike. It was going to bring sneaker culture back to basketball. The feedback was solid and interaction on social media showed a lot of promise when the shoe first appeared.

When Launch/Release Day arrived, the dialogue around the Kyrie 6 hinted that it would be on fire. I took a look at the Kyrie 6 three days after the release date. Three days is a short release window and shouldn't really be used as a measuring stick, but the basic Black/White Kyrie 6 colorway was built up to be something special.

The 3 day window is important because it shows the shift in how long a new release remains *hot* in the public eye. Ten years ago a new release could be hot for weeks and maintain a resale value. This is how I operated my Amazon store. I would go to Foot Locker, or other retail stores, ask about sizes and make the shoes available on my Amazon store. As the shoes sold I would go and pick them up. It was great. Each new release gave me a two week window to earn.

As the years passed that two week window shortened by two days each year. In 2017 that window was still about 5 days, but StockX introduced a new wrinkle. By 2019 I couldn't really look at new releases as an option for resale. Three days is now plenty of time to determine if a new release will be a solid release for a retailer. In this instance the Kyrie 6 had 3 days and on Footlocker and Hibbett

Sports websites there wasn't a single broken size. Jimmy Jazz had a couple of broken sizes, but the third party site StockX, after three days, showed a data set disheartening to traditional retail and ecommerce.

The obvious process of analysis should be that three days was far too soon to expect broken sizes a week prior to Black Friday. The doorbuster deals and the hyped sneaker releases that arrived, the closer we moved towards "holiday" shopping, created the unfortunate problem of "holding" for customers in the market. The Kyrie 6 was being released within 20 days of the Air Jordan 11 Retro Bred, but the Kyrie releases have always been dropped around Christmas, and around the annual Jordan 11 releases. The first two releases of the Kyrie Series had substantial sell through. Sales were so good *the Kyrie 1 and 2 ranked in the top 10 shoes sold* according to the NPD Group[1] at a time when basketball signature sneakers were trending down. The Kyrie 3 was when the model began to cool off. Let's get back to the Kyrie 6 release.

---

[1] https://www.npd.com/wps/portal/npd/us/home/ the primary source of information on point of sales data for the sneaker industry

The mentions and excitement for the Kyrie 6 were considerable and with the way social media and mentions are being regarded in marketing, the Kyrie at $130.00 should have seen some sell through and broken sizes, but that wasn't the case. What is the case is that three days after the release StockX showed 94 shoes sold at 22.3% below the retail price and an average sale price of $123.00. For this to take place there are only two things that could be happening:

1. Retail outlets are selling their inventory on StockX
2. Sellers with discounts are selling their inventory on StockX

In either case StockX has unintentionally set the price of the Kyrie at below retail and this shapes retail as the site garners as much traffic as both Hibbett/City Gear and Jimmy Jazz combined; and more than Footlocker as direct competition. (November 2019)

Website: Traffic

- StockX: 15.79 Million/month

- Hibbett/City Gear: 3.80 Million/month

- Footlocker: 10.87 Million/month

- Jimmy Jazz: 2.47 Million/month

I have been writing on my website that resale is dead at retail. This should mean that StockX shouldn't have had any sales. StockX is a resale site. Someone has to make the product available. Unless store accounts are selling the product, where are the shoes coming from that are being sold below retail? Remember the $130 SRP is before taxes and the average sold on StockX was $123. StockX takes their 11-14% which means that the seller is only getting a $109.47-$105.78 return. The SRP is 130.00!

StockX is intriguing. It is both an indicator of how poorly the Kyrie 6 performed out of the gates in general release and an indicator of where the market wants the Kyrie 6 to be priced.

This leads to a discussion on StockX vs traditional retail. The Suggested Retail Price is really the price wholesale accounts have to sell the shoe for before they can mark it down. Nike does not allow retailers to sell shoes at a discount within the first few weeks of release. Since retailers are 'stuck' at 130.00, they are faced with the reality that this model has a baseline set below retail via StockX. The consumer does not have any motivation to pay 130.00 for the shoe if by evidence of StockX's last five sales (in November 2019 when I originally researched this), the price was dropping considerably per pair:

Size	Sale Price	Date	Time
8	$101	Sunday, November 24, 2019	11:25 PM EST
10.5	$95	Sunday, November 24, 2019	6:07 PM EST
10	$101	Sunday, November 24, 2019	12:44 PM EST
10	$109	Sunday, November 24, 2019	11:24 AM EST
8	$101	Sunday, November 24, 2019	10:13 AM EST

The average price of the last 5 sales was 101.40

The value of the Kyrie trended down. The model is now at an average price of $81.00 dollars/pair in 2020, less than six months from release. I do understand that every customer isn't shopping on StockX and that speed of delivery is an issue when a customer purchases on StockX, but traditional retail is in the awkward position in the first week of release of having to answer questions about price matching in-store because of prices online. StockX is becoming more popular every day. Even during the COVID-19 crisis, the site remained open while most sneaker brands and retailers closed.

The company is advertising on national television, during Super Bowl games and sponsoring an NBA team. Retail outlets who pricematch (the process of beating a competitor's price) are no longer capable of price matching online retail. Many retail locations now price match stores in the same location/mall only.

StockX holds an unfair advantage that actually contributes to the devaluation of footwear and this hurts all parties involved. Writing that last sentence bothers me. How can StockX have an unfair advantage if it doesn't carry inventory? The company doesn't have the burden of buying kicks wholesale and storing kicks. The company only has authenticators and people to ship the shoes out.

Retail outlets almost function as warehousing for brands. There isn't an opportunity for a retailer to create a marketplace that allows customers to make a bid at the price they desire. Brands wouldn't accept this from their wholesale accounts. So… how does StockX have an unfair advantage? This leads me to ask the question:

Should StockX implement an SRP first week policy of *retail offers only* for sellers?

This removes the open marketplace concept that StockX was founded upon. But, *buybacks* and *sell-offs* that take place in the stock market are often meant as a correction in most instances. If StockX is supposed to be comparable to the actual stock market who or what creates the regulations? The SEC monitors the stock market. No one monitors a private business, which leads to inherent problems on the StockX platform.

On StockX when a general release model is in 'sell off' mode in the first week of release, it creates an issue. The low price that StockX had on the Kyrie contributes indirectly to the backlog of inventory at retail and contributes to inflated prices on more coveted commodities. StockX doesn't hold any responsibility in making this adjustment. The company earns if the shoe sells for 1 dollar or 1000, but when a general release consistently fails to generate resale from retail, StockX is in danger of cannibalizing itself, or am I wrong?

Should StockX self-regulate to improve their marketplace? This self-regulation would improve retail which has been in a tailspin since brick and mortar stores decided promotions could help clear inventory. SRP can only hold in today's sneaker marketplace when the shoe is a limited release or hyped product. That isn't a healthy environment. I ask again, should StockX self-regulate?

It isn't reasonable for me to request regulation of a private company, but retailers are in a difficult position. Brands are looking at StockX's ability to generate interest and traffic and they are aligning with the site to launch product.

Did you catch that?

Retailers used to be the first place that brands sent product. This shifted as direct-to-consumer has grown. Today brands have the ability to reach almost 20 million customers at one time working with StockX. That won't happen if a retailer launched an exclusive product with a store like *Shoe Palace*.

Consider New Balance did a launch with Shoe Palace featuring Kawhi Leonard. The launch was regional and took place in California. California has 45 Shoe Palace stores. The average number of shoes a store gets in a limited release is around 48 pair. Kawhi is in Los Angeles. The Clippers are not the biggest team in the state. That honor belongs to the Lakers and the Golden State Warriors. The assumption can be made that a limited release at 45 stores wasn't really what happened, but if it did and each store got 48 pair, that's 2,160 shoes. Those shoes had to be moved through the supply chain and shipped to each individual location.

Now consider this, Adidas did a launch with StockX. It wasn't regional; it hit everyone with the app on their phone or the site bookmarked on their laptop. In the next two chapters I am going to introduce you to the fact that brands are recognizing the value of

StockX. The collaboration between adidas Campus 80s MakerLab x StockX is an example of how a brand can sell 999 pair in three days using StockX; no supply chain needed.

This creates a serious issue for traditional retail.

To be honest, this chapter isn't really about regulating StockX. It's intended to open your eyes to how one website has so drastically changed the retail landscape in the sneaker industry.

Chapter

2

Why Retailers Needed the adidas MakerLab Limited-Edition Campus 80s x StockX IPO to be Flawed

Honoring its ongoing ambition to elevate creators worldwide, adidas presents Campus 80s MakerLab , the next chapter of the brand's collaborative-creation platform that unleashes unlimited possibilities

Source: [adidas MakerLab propels emerging designers to bring limited-edition Campus 80s Into the Global Marketplace](#)[2]

When Josh Luber started StockX the immediate idea behind the company was to truly become a stock market of things. As the company moved in scale and in valuation he announced over and over

---

[2] [adidas MakerLab propels emerging designers to bring limited-edition Campus 80s Into the Global Marketplace](#)

that the endgame was to be a place where the fair market value of a product could be delivered through an IPO for new products. There have been several successful launches of these IPOs with a LeBron x Cleveland Cavs Homecourt IPO and a Ben Baller Slide IPO. Both of these "events" were for extremely limited items. This adidas collaboration is interesting because DTC has shifted the relationship between retail and brands. adidas created another hard shift by making this MakerLab drop happen in conjunction with a third party marketplace. I don't want to get confusing, so let me slow down and explain the adidas x StockX release.

From adidas and StockX:

In a first for MakerLab, 333 limited-edition pairs of each model will launch via a StockX IPO on October 15th, 2019. The IPO model bridges the conversation between creator and buyer, removing bots, campouts, raffles, or plugs, and empowering the buyer to set the retail price.

The 72-hour auction will begin **21:00 EDT, October 15th** and run through **21:00 EDT, October 18th** where users can select their preferred designs and size on the platform. Through a blind bid, each consumer will offer how much they are willing to pay for their selected model of the [Campus 80s](). Winners, or highest bidders, will all secure the shoes at the "Clearing Price" or the lowest winning Bid on a specific size and design of the shoe.

The IPO will **close at 21:00 EDT** on **Friday, October 18, 2019** with the highest winning bids matched by availability.

The goal of a limited drop should be to generate interest across the brand, and to gain enough coverage that people who usually wouldn't hear about a drop from a brand will take interest and it will contribute to new fans of the brand. That should be the goal. The reality is limited releases usually cater to the niche fashion or sneaker enthusiast.

Why should retailers have wanted this launch to be flawed?

StockX has grown in scope through the continuous advertisement of the site for customer acquisitions. The site now reaches a different consumer. This new demographic for StockX isn't really interested in hyped shoes, but they are interested in bargains. I can say this because of the drop in the average transaction price from my own data. The drop in the *average sales price per transaction* indicates that a different consumer is visiting the site. Where the site originally drove engagement at the high end with sneakerheads looking for hard to find drops, the site has become a haven for clearance items. The amount of shoes being sold below retail and at deep discounts is clear evidence that people are not looking to StockX as only a "hyped" shoe release platform solely.

I made the argument that the shift in consumers on the site created a few issues for StockX. I assumed the people who were going to look at this IPO are not the same people who only ten months ago set the average price for a pair of slides[3] at, *"10,000 Bids on the*

---

[3] https://stockx.com/news/ben-baller-ipo-results/

800 slides listed, and because of the unique pricing method, using our take on a blind dutch auction, the black slides sold at an average Clearing Price of $181 and the red at $260."

In <u>August I wrote a report on</u>[4] my average price per transaction on StockX. In the post I explained that:

In my book, <u>Nike's Consumer Direct Offense, Amazon and StockX: The Disruption of Sneaker Retail</u>[5], I shared my per transaction for 2018. Here is the paragraph from the book.

$583,244 / 4270 = $136.59 ... StockX has shifted demographics. The site is no longer pulling in people because of shoes that have hit resale, or are limited; the site is capturing sales on a considerable amount of "non-sneakerhead" shoes listed on the site. I happen to think the least expensive shoes sold could be higher from 30-100, but the site does not list a lot of shoes.

The last sentence needs to be explained because it is out of context. StockX has a complex system for creating product listings. Because the seller isn't able to create a listing, if a shoe isn't on the site, information has to be submitted for the shoe to be listed. This is a

---

[4] https://arch-usa.com/the-democratization-of-sneaker-resale/
[5] https://amzn.to/2zcCNmj

process that can take from a day to a week. It limits the amount of shoes on the site. The rest of the quote about the average transaction for my account at $136.59/pair is explained in the following paragraph.

In 2017 my average transaction was 170 dollars a pair. In 2019 my numbers for August saw the average transaction at around 87 dollars per pair. If I take the average of all of my sales on StockX since I hit 1 million dollars in 18 months the numbers are really interesting. I hit 1 million dollars in sales on June 22nd, 2019. It took 18 months. Since June 22nd my sales were $253,632.00 for 2019 (half a year) at an average price of $119.58.

This fluctuation in prices happened for a number of reasons. Let's get back to why I made the claim that retailers should have wanted the adidas x StockX IPO to be flawed.

Two reasons:

1. My summer transactions decreased to 87 dollars due to the typical slowdown before school. The increase back to 119 was due to back-to-school. A site like StockX should never shift according to traditional shopping seasons since the premise of

the site is that a customer can find limited release items. This underscores a serious issue that no one is really addressing. StockX's consumer is shifting.

2. adidas has retail partners they are ignoring to release a shoe with a website that doesn't have an account with the brand. StockX is not a retail outlet. A shoe that is limited should always be given to the wholesale partners who have been working hard to move adidas' product. Unless adidas has limited release product in the pipeline for their retail accounts the brand could find itself falling out of favor with buyers. Since October, adidas hasn't utilized StockX for another drop, so my commentary here is basically a prediction. Retail should prepare for more of these releases. This is also important, if adidas places limited releases into the hands of its best retail accounts when the shoe sells out the store could gain residual sales from visitors to the store helping to clear older inventory. This is the type of event that creates an experience. adidas is giving StockX an experiential marketing event which is unheard of for a third party/online resale platform. A resale channel doesn't really have the ability to build experiences. At

its core it is simply a destination to purchase what you can't find. adidas created an experience for third party. That should be troubling.

As popular as StockX has become, and although I state that the site is functioning like traditional retail, the site is still not as popular or as prominent as it could be.

When I originally wrote parts of this section it was prior to the adidas IPO.

In the next chapter the reality of what happened should have been much more discussed in the sneaker industry, but it wasn't and still hasn't been discussed… until now.

Chapter

3

10 Reasons the 'adidas Campus 80s x StockX IPO' Was the Most Important Drop of the Year

Here is your official recap of the adidas Campus 80s StockX IPO. Source: [The adidas Campus 80s StockX IPO Recap – StockX News](#)[6]

When I discovered that StockX and adidas were aligning to create a launch that was conceived and born strictly on StockX's website I wrote that the collab between adidas and StockX was not going to work. I gave compelling data to suggest that StockX's market had shifted to fewer sneakerheads and more mainstream customers. The article is linked below and shared in the footnotes:

[Why the adidas MakerLab Limited-Edition Campus 80s x StockX IPO is Flawed for Both StockX and adidas](#)[7]

---

[6] https://stockx.com/news/adidas-campus-80s-ipo-recap/
[7] https://arch-usa.com/why-the-adidas-makerlab-limited-edition-campus-80s-x-stockx-ipo-is-flawed-for-both-stockx-and-adidas

The previous chapter is a modified version of that website post. In the original article I said that the launch was flawed, but the reality is I wanted people to read my post and understand what it meant for small retailers and small chains already dealing with the Nike Consumer Direct Offense issues. I wanted the launch to be flawed because,

If ... this IPO went off without any problems and was successful it could become a case study for how adidas would be able to shift their release options away from under-performing brick and mortar accounts.

That's not a bad thing for adidas to be fair. If a brick and mortar is having trouble selling adidas products, then this is the first domino to fall in creating a promotional environment.

I hoped the IPO was flawed and that it would fall flat. Traditional retail is already facing considerable pressure from every brand's direct-to-consumer growth. If adidas, who hasn't clearly stated or introduced a term for their strategy for DTC/growth (this doesn't mean that adidas isn't growing DTC), but if adidas finds a partner in StockX it could send another shot through traditional retail.

StockX is a private company so <u>the report they just wrote on the IPO could be skewed</u>[8]. I'm not in a position to pull back the curtain, but to build a case for why this collaboration between a brand and third party site is so important, I made a few comments and predictions to create dialogue since I wasn't able to find other sites looking at the seriousness of an *all-digital* launch from a major brand to a third party platform.

According to StockX the IPO was a success. That makes this launch a harbinger. adidas' play has given all of retail a textbook for working with a digital outlet. adidas' StockX collaboration gave the Three Stripes the value of releasing 3000 pair vs the actual 999 pairs dropped.

Get it? If you don't I'm giving you a list here of why this partnership is extremely important for business discussions.

---

[8] https://stockx.com/news/adidas-campus-80s-ipo-recap/

10 Reasons Why This Was the Biggest Drop of the Year

1. The Campus series like the Continental 80, Samba and Stan Smith, retails at between 80-100 dollars. If we look at the newest model of adidas' *under 100* shoes, the Continental, we find a model that didn't perform very well for the brand. The shoes are on considerable markdown. You can grab the Continental 80 at both urban and traditional retail stores for 29.99 a pair (9.99 with a 20 dollar VIP coupon). While adidas continues to take market share, it has slowed considerably from its explosive 2014-2017 growth. This has created a problem for all adidas models due to a glut of inventory at wholesale accounts.

2. adidas didn't just hit a wall at retail in 2017 in North America, they lost the wall. In 2015 and 2016 adidas dominated wholesale accounts so much that Jordan Brand was pushed to the back of the wall and adidas was given the front of the store in Finish Line and Foot Locker stores. Today adidas has been shifted to the back of the store. Nike is back at the front of the store and the adidas wall has been reduced to make room for

Vans, Fila and New Balance. I have to add that saying this creates a paradox. Adidas since 2015 has added 8 billion to their gross revenue. I'll get into this a bit later.

3. adidas' Pharrell products the adilette and Solar Hu releases are following the Tennis Hu drops from Pharrell and sitting. The endorsers of adidas are no longer delivering sale through like they did a few years ago when scarcity was king.

4. Above I wrote that the StockX IPO generated the value of releasing **3000 pair of shoes**. The number of pairs is not significant, but when you consider research done by [Housakicks on Yeezy drops before adidas](https://housakicks.com/buy-it-now/adidas-yeezy-powerphase-core-black-how-many-made-buy-it-now/)[9] began releasing the products in large numbers they were dropping 2000 pair of Yeezy at a time. If StockX agreed to this IPO at seller level 4 for adidas, they charged adidas 11% per transaction. When adidas sells a drop to retailers they are at 50%. **adidas possibly netted 89%** on a drop through a third party digital outlet. There wasn't a traditional supply chain involved. The shoes were created and shipped straight to the customer at a markup up from the retail of 80 bucks for a Campus to this price,

---

[9] https://housakicks.com/buy-it-now/adidas-yeezy-powerphase-core-black-how-many-made-buy-it-now/

"**Across all three sneakers, the average clearing price was $205, and the average number of Bids was 3308**" (StockX).

5. That 3308 number is for each individual colorway which means adidas could have possibly sold 10,000 pair of shoes in this drop. If you're a retailer reading this, especially a small retail outlet, this is more than the allotment of shoes you receive from adidas in a general release. The scariest part of this is StockX hasn't even hit the growth that it could reach.

6. The StockX IPO could open the door for something I discussed in my last book, adidas could plan a series of IPOs throughout the year with StockX and StockX could function as a fulfillment center. This removes inventory from adidas' coffers and allows for a seamless experience for StockX shoppers who often worry about fakes. The shoes wouldn't have to be authenticated expediting the speed of delivery taking away the one wall StockX has in customer satisfaction.

7. adidas created this drop in the Makers Lab. This means that a product was conceived, designed and launched in under 3 months. The traditional production process for footwear is 6

months to a year. As I've already stated the shoe never had to ship to wholesale accounts. While this isn't DTC, it's about the closest thing to DTC.

8. Retail outlets are notorious for backdoor relationships that leave customers frustrated. This launch was even across the board. Everyone wasn't going to win, but bots were useless. Yes, the price of the shoe is prohibitive for the everyday consumer, moms buying kicks for their kids, but that is not the point here. This was a strategy to drive adidas sales at the high end. Which leads me to one of the biggest points:

9. **adidas just had a *Yeezy drop moment without Yeezy*.** The rapper/designer/businessman is erratic and relying on Yeezy to create the narrative of adidas places the company in a precarious position. The brand just found a way to bring the focus back to the brand and the designers. Had adidas simply used their own platform to launch this designer series, it would not have accomplished the same results. This would have been a slow sell through because adidas lacks the internal structure for storytelling and reaching the customer willing to pay 205 dollars for an 80 dollar pair of kicks not named Yeezy.

10. I've repeated this throughout, not one retail outlet was needed to sell a limited release product not attached to a famous entertainer or athlete. In my previous book I stated that retailers needed to begin functioning like brands. Since they don't have their own private labels to create stories around, they need to create content for all of the brands they carry. StockX delivered the story of the shoe via their news section on the site. They then carried the story to their social media pages. They built interest around the products with engaging content and imagery. If StockX had a physical location they would have had a line for an adidas shoe made by Helen Kirkum... Helen Kirkum ain't Ye and she didn't have to be... and this could happen every month and it wouldn't burn out the masses. The IPO report was written on October 23rd. Since then the Kirkum 80 has been resold at a markup of 162.8% above retail. The demand for the model is still there... The demand is still there.

I'm not saying this is as big as Nike's CDO, but an *all-digital* drop happened without any big names attached to it on a model that retails for 80 dollars.

StockX is becoming an example of what retail e-commerce could have been and during the COVID-19 crisis it establishes what I've been saying for years. Retailers failed to become media companies and relied on the old *post and sell it* method to capture online shoppers. Amazon is the only site capable of pulling off this old, flat, white background picture format for selling. All other stores need to realize the consumer is best served when they are educated and entertained and even then the policies that StockX has created has empowered the platform in a way that regular retail, because it followed Amazon, simply can't do.

StockX has made a platform where returns are non-existent. Later in this book I will discuss the opportunity for retail to adjust and create a new experience using returns, but right now I have to focus on how StockX has created the perfect model, so much so that the company is becoming just as bulletproof as Nike in a way.

Last year StockX encountered an issue that happens to all internet sites. The site was hacked. This hack was substantial and could have led to the defection of sellers from the platform, but it didn't. Sellers on StockX are constantly complaining about the low offers on the site and the sellers who list products for cheap. Browse YouTube and you can find hundreds of videos on all of the problems. When the hack took place, sneaker culture enthusiasts made videos and wrote articles on how the site was about to die. I countered with my own thoughts on why the hack was not enough to make sellers walk away.

Chapter

4

Why the Hack of StockX Didn't Hurt?

As StockX reached Unicorn status, Josh Luber stepped down as CEO of the company he created. This happened at the end of June 2019. However, according to Tech Crunch, "An unnamed data breached seller contacted TechCrunch claiming more than 6.8 million records were stolen from the site in May by a hacker. The seller declined to say how they obtained the data."

When investments occur all information must be disclosed to avoid the perception of impropriety. At the time the question that should have been asked is if the "$110 million in a Series C funding round led by DST Global, General Atlantic and GGV Capital," (Forbes) should be retracted? This question never came up.

The question users should have had was what exactly was stolen and should the credit cards associated with StockX accounts be cancelled? There were a host of other questions, but my primary question when the hack happened was if a seller like me (over a million dollars in 18 months) wasn't notified, and I'm not saying I'm more important than a kid who only sold or bought one pair, doesn't this hint at the fragility of the third party marketplace?

To be honest any marketplace created has been hacked before. Here is a post on Amazon:

https://www.hackread.com/amazon-suffers-security-breach/[10]

This is an article on eBay:

https://www.cnet.com/news/ebay-hacked-requests-all-users-change-passwords/[11]

From Amazon to eBay, hacking remains a constant threat to anyone who has made the effort to join the ranks of online business. My own site carried a hack in its header that I had to purchase several programs to fix. The hack resulted in a problem when someone shared a link from my site; the information that showed up was for a casino. The hack has been cleaned and wasn't harmful. There wasn't any malicious code, but it is one of the reasons why my e-commerce store is

---

[10] https://www.hackread.com/amazon-suffers-security-breach/
[11] https://www.cnet.com/news/ebay-hacked-requests-all-users-change-passwords/

no longer active as the place I sell. I just didn't feel comfortable building an e-commerce platform. This is what makes a site like Stadium Goods such an amazing third party platform. The time and effort to build a site where everything relies on the owner of the site is extremely difficult.

I changed my e-commerce store to an affiliate site. This was a bonus a couple of years ago. It used to make a nice amount of money by forwarding buyers to Amazon and eBay, but now that most third party sales take place on StockX, my online store helps drives search and discovery to my store and site, but the amount of affiliate income has dropped.

There is an opportunity for me here to discuss how StockX has disrupted affiliate revenue for sneaker sales, but that's a different discussion. Let's get back to my own hack to establish why the hack of StockX is concerning, but isn't enough to stop sellers from utilizing the platform, or buyers.

I shut down my store because I didn't want customers registering for the site to worry about their data. I chose to sell through StockX first as an experiment and then because it was so damn easy.

Although I tell anyone who will listen to establish their own site before joining a third party to sell their footwear, I sell on StockX because the site has given me benefits that aren't granted to everyday sellers because of the amount of sneakers I've sold. When the hack of StockX happened I realized that being a big seller with a personal representative on StockX means very little as no one reached out to tell me anything in May 2019. The company didn't even explain all of the issues that were affecting the site after the hack. When they sent out a password update request, I didn't even think to ask why because it was back to school season and my sales on the platform had skyrocketed, remember the average per transaction increase in Chapter 2? That kept me busy and I overlooked the hack.

I eventually wrote my rep to ask what was happening and it took a few days for her to respond. At the time I saw StockX as a fragile unicorn. A business, built on the backs of sellers, that is only as strong as those sellers making a decision to remain sellers. The hack provided an opportunity to pull together funding and establish an opponent to StockX and other sites. The collection of sellers I know could immediately be a 10 million dollar a year company.

I didn't do anything though.

I didn't contact any other sellers locally, Memphis has a number of VIP sellers on StockX, so I could have organized something, but the hack became a blip on my radar. I've grown accustomed to my early payout on StockX and so has everyone else.

This unfortunately means one thing… the hack was newsworthy, but ultimately no one I know left the platform. I once thought of StockX as a fragile unicorn. I still think that if retailers understood the importance of becoming media companies and creating interactive e-commerce and digital platforms, StockX could be very fragile.

After the adidas Campus 80s x StockX launch and StockX's ability to continue operating through the COVID-19 crisis, StockX and sites like *GOAT, The RealReal* and *Stadium Goods* contribute to the shaping of retail in a way that allows for a new conversation about what retail should and could be, but it's not straightforward.

A quick look at two of these third party retail sites, *The RealReal* and *StockX* could provide more insight into the topic of new retail before this book turns towards how brands and retailers have to consider: wholesale accounts, DTC by brands, and the digital experience when preparing to relaunch after the Coronavirus.

I will continue to reiterate that the new industry built on resale e-commerce should not exist if retailers had adapted digital strategies as brands pivoted to DTC. To make the statement, 'companies with billion dollar valuations shouldn't exist' I need to explain why they exist.

Chapter

5

10 Reasons the RealReal IPO and StockX's Unicorn Status Happened

The RealReal had not made a profit before it launched an IPO[12]. The site, a secondhand market for authentic luxury goods, exists in the same lane as *What Goes Around Comes Around*, a secondhand business that currently has store-within-stores at big box retailer Dillards. During a crisis like COVID-19 luxury is the first thing to take a hit, for obvious reasons, but both StockX and The RealReal are companies operating as tech middlemen. When they are both valued at these huge numbers, it shows that a businesses' worth doesn't exactly reflect common sense.

---

[12] Luxury second-hand site The RealReal sees stock jump 45% after IPO
https://www.cbsnews.com/news/the-realreal-luxury-consignment-site-secondhand-marketplace-ipo-stock-jumps-45-percent/

The RealReal didn't turn a profit, but was able to IPO and generate over 300 Million in their launch. They lost $76 million in 2018 and $42 million the year before.

StockX attained a billion dollar valuation. The co-founder stepped down and an eBay exec steps in. This is a sign that StockX may be preparing for an IPO as well.

The question is why and how are online sites generating these fantastic valuations doing so without turning a profit? While StockX is a private company and information on the income is not readily available, the amount of advertising, the number of employees, and the fact that, like Amazon, their shipping and receiving is operating at a loss, gives a clear picture that StockX's valuation is rooted in its software and users. StockX has one of the most accessible UX/CX experiences on the market and the site could easily shift into other areas.

In the source article on The RealReal it states,

Poshmark, an online retailer of secondhand clothing, expanded earlier this month into home decor with items including bedding and bath. Online rival ThredUP is opening physical stores.

Meanwhile, Neiman Marcus in April 2019 bought a minority stake in resale site Fashionphile. As part of this deal, at select Neiman Marcus stores, customers are able to not only receive an immediate quote for their items from Fashionphile but also payments they can spend immediately on new luxury items at the store. Traditional retail, as I mentioned with Dillard's and *What Goes Around*, is adapting by trying to become like digital and new retail outlets. Acquisition and investment is not innovation and big box retail won't survive by adding startups to their coffers.

In my previous book, *Nike's Consumer Direct Offense, Amazon & StockX: The Disruption of Sneaker Retail*, I discussed that StockX only has two eventual options, acquisition by eBay or add categories to eventually IPO. I made this prediction because of my own experiences with Amazon and e-commerce, but I also made a statement that I want to reiterate now:

The RealReal and StockX shouldn't exist but they do exist because established retail is failing at innovating and storytelling.

eBay and Amazon are the original reseller locations, but these new third party platforms were able to creep into the market because where eBay and Amazon saw flaws in retail, StockX and The RealReal saw flaws in eBay and Amazon. Business is about disruption. Things that are new and shiny catch the eye and invite users. Why and how are The RealReal and StockX here? They are here because retail has failed to adapt at the physical and digital levels.

As this book moves towards a discussion on how retail will have to relaunch into a world shaken to its core by a virus, serious conversations will have to take place. I want to start with ten reasons how two companies that own **no inventory** have been able to do what they've done:

1. Retail is stagnant.

2. Leasing and square footage isn't being maximized.

3. Brands are making bigger steps towards DTC.

4. Retail has failed to realize that personalization, professionalism, product knowledge and customer service, are not minimum wage skills.

5. Discounts don't drive loyalty.

6. Quality inspires loyalty.

7. Storytelling is important.

8. Fast fashion is a lie.

9. Relying on the brand is lazy.

10. The "urban" consumer is going digital.

Retail is in a precarious position and the dialogue around the industry is owned by people with data who haven't worked in the stores and are lacking firsthand experience with the shift.

StockX and The RealReal shouldn't have a place in the patheon of "billion" dollar businesses, but they do. The strange thing is ThredUp, Grailed, GOAT, and Poshmark are more popular than established stores and chains with 50-100 locations, which speaks volumes about why brands are looking at digital as the new wholesale.

Here is a dangerous hypothetical based on the adidas x StockX 80s launch. Right now brands are discovering the power of direct to consumer. They aren't really discovering this; they are simply making sure to utilize technology to build a bridge to their consumer that wasn't there in the past. The internet is the great equalizer, but it can also be considered the great decimator. The internet is an unwitting Death Star, a devourer of planets. That's not quite right because the internet is not a living thing. The internet is a tool.

adidas was able to utilize StockX to launch a product. What happens if other brands follow suit? You're talking about removing aspects of the supply chain that have long been a staple of retail. Traditionally the brand makes a product, buyers check it out and then the brand ships the product to the warehouse of the retail outlet. The retailer then has to get the product to its doors. As I mentioned earlier all of those steps were removed with a digital warehouse auction on StockX. The removal of the traditional supply chain doesn't happen if StockX doesn't prove that it can successfully drive engagement.

StockX and The RealReal are doing things to reach consumers that traditional retail isn't doing. These *fragile* ideas realized their shortcomings and they are doing something about it. This has given both businesses growth and access, to the detriment of long time businesses in the same category. Just how are these companies luring in customers when the product in many cases is within driving distance of the consumer?

Digitally native brands and companies are using intelligent marketing strategies to move beyond advertising to *only* their target demographics.

Chapter

6

StockX Buying Ad Time During the WNBA Season is More Important Than it Looks

StockX has removed itself from my opinion that the company is fragile by creating one of the most efficient e-commerce platforms in the industry.

The return rate on StockX is *nothing*. This is its most valuable asset to a seller. Right now every brand that has decided to go direct-to-consumer is dealing with inventory issues and returns. Nike is building new facilities to handle their returns. DTC is smart, but as I mentioned when I said the hack of StockX proved the company is bulletproof, I sell on that channel because I don't have to worry about returns. In my previous book I explained how sneaker returns on Amazon were around 30% and how that damaged my business. StockX is an interesting platform because the people who shop there don't get to have buyer's remorse. There isn't any other sneaker outlet that has this benefit. It's an invaluable quality and one that you would assume would limit the site. It hasn't.

The site is continuing to grow at a rate that is impressive because usually after about two years the growth of a site tapers off. In October 2019 StockX was getting 15.8 Million visitors a month. Today, through the COVID-19 crisis the site is now averaging 18.36 Million visitors a month. This is because the platform recognizes that it is a tech middleman. StockX's growth has forced eBay to take the site more seriously (this will be discussed later), but eBay had to adjust because as I've continuously stated, StockX is finding new customers. StockX is moving itself from a niche business to the mainstream.

The StockX commercial "Buy and Sell Sneakers and Streetwear"[13] originally launched in November of 2018. The spot doesn't feature any famous people. The commercial does include a lot of famous kicks; which makes it appear that the ad is targeted to 'sneakerheads' but with the shifting nature of the consumption of me-

---

[13] https://www.youtube.com/watch?v=cqzu-71W3SA&feature=emb_title

dia by young people and the fact that the ad originally aired at the start of the NBA season, who was really the target for the ad?

On YouTube or social where the spot has aired, the obvious target is teens and young adults who know what "Grails" are, but StockX is doing something in the commercial that I stated was happening via sales I've made on the site. StockX is no longer a hypebeast/sneakerhead destination only.

A quick note from Forbes during the 2019 finals, "So far this season, the WNBA has seen a 36 percent increase in viewership in adults age 18 to 49, a 29 percent jump in men in that age group and a 50 percent increase in women. Through June, WNBA games on ESPN2 are averaging 250,000 viewers, a 39 percent improvement from last year and the best start for the league since 2013. The June 28 game between the Sparks and the Seattle Storm drew 378,000 viewers. It was the most watched regular season WNBA game on ESPN2 since 2011."

This is where things get interesting for a company like StockX vs the competition. StockX aired the commercial at the start of the NBA season. The average age of the NBA viewer is 42. While watching the Seattle Storm vs the Connecticut Sun during the 2019 season the spot aired and immediately I realized that StockX is not settling for hype. I already understood this as my data from selling on StockX in 2018, showed that almost a quarter of my sales were under 100 dollars on shoes that were not "grails".

An ad spot for footwear and apparel during live sports doesn't really relate to the IG crowd. Kids aren't really sports fans the way my generation was and still is. Sports fanaticism in the U.S. is centered around the college experience in many cases and around the aspirations of kids who want to be pro athletes. The people, who watch sports, either played, wanted to play or cheer on their alma maters and athletes who come from their schools. In other words demographics of sports fans are completely different than the people who StockX was originally created to reach: the resale market.

Yet, on a Sunday afternoon on ABC during a WNBA game StockX was running a commercial telling those watching, "Now You Know" and for me it was evidence that StockX is willing to spend the dollars to find their next customer. It is also evidence that StockX is paying attention to women just like brands are beginning to pay attention to women. Advertising is something accounts with 100+ brick and mortar locations aren't doing and are incapable of doing and that's a threat. It's also something larger retail outlets for sneakers aren't doing and again, that's a threat.

StockX, like Uber, doesn't have inventory. It is completely reliant on third party. That third party traditionally acquired inventory from urban accounts and traditional retailers. As brands become more invested in DTC the third party sellers on a platform like StockX are acquiring their inventory from brand doors. StockX is only one shift away from creating a 'Fulfillment' for brands and possibly opening their own doors in 'key cities' throughout the U.S. While I touched on this briefly in my last book, the more I see where and how StockX is advertising the more I realize how quickly the footwear industry is moving.

The ad that ran in 2018 was followed by an increase in output by StockX on its YouTube station. In traditional retail the only company really ramping up the output of content is Foot Locker. Jimmy Jazz is also doing a good job of ramping up content creation. Foot Locker is on another level. They run a "Season of Greatness" campaign every year and they recently acquired NTWRK and launched a platform named Greenhouse. Both of these sites are content driven sales platforms who are targeted towards the IG community. Foot Locker advertising to the IG crowd makes sense because parents already know about Foot Locker, but the sneakerhead crowd is moving towards StockX, Stadium Goods and GOAT. Foot Locker obviously took care of itself by investing in GOAT, but other retailers, smaller chains, aren't taking advantage of media and they aren't capable of acquiring a startup like GOAT.

To be fair the sneaker industry is a multibillion dollar industry and my focus on StockX could be considered trivial. However, it's easy to overlook things as niche until they begin to shape retail. I've made the statement that StockX made itself more than just a resale platform and in doing so they removed themselves from my 'fragile' unicorn opinion, but the reality is everything can be disrupted and it's clear that shifts happen more quickly than they ever have.

How can StockX be disrupted and what exactly is being done right now to push back at the growing resale market that has disrupted traditional retail? What can be done if a company is reemerging after COVID-19 and potentially coming back from bankruptcy? It's important to look at all aspects to create a more in depth discussion.

Chapter

7

Nike's Supply Chain as Disruptor

"Nike's anti-theft buckle is different from all previous sneaker anti-theft buckles. This time, Nike's anti-theft buckle contains RFID tags and uses RFID technology."[14]

The quote above is from an article discussing Nike's continued investment in their Consumer Direct Offense by improving methods of detecting counterfeit products.

I wrote a chapter in my previous book on the value of StockX, not as an authentication service and a middleman, but for their software. In the book I explained that investment into consignment

---

[14] https://www.nfctagfactory.com/news/Nike-will-introduce-RFID-as-a-new-means-of-after-sales-counterfeit-detection.html

businesses, while extremely attractive on the surface have underlying issues that make any long term investment very shaky.

Why did I make this claim when StockX recently attained 'unicorn' status and GOAT was given a 100 Million dollar investment?

Because of a basic eye test…

GOAT and StockX aren't valuable because they can authenticate shoes, they are valuable because they built an incredible user base and an exciting interface that improves on the customer experience for visitors to those apps versus the experience customers have when they visit Foot Locker or other brick and mortar e-commerce. Customer experience and a great user interface still fails to make clear why I've said that authentication services are shaky. When I say authentication services I'm talking sites like GOAT, StockX, The RealReal and What Goes Around. These businesses *appear* to be built on the value placed in authentication, but if this is the case then the back and forth I've been writing about in regard to saying these businesses are fragile is valid because both adidas and Nike have begun to take steps to help their customers with authenticating products.

On my site a year ago I explained that adidas already uses RFID in their hangtags.

adidas' keen interest in monitoring it's footwear via RFID has allowed adidas since 2015 to keep better track of their inventory and this, along with improved product and marketing, has enabled the brand to add 8 Billion dollars to their gross income.

Up until last year Nike wasn't monitoring their inventory via RFID, but that changed as Nike rolled out a new label format. The new label has both RFID and QR Codes. RFID was introduced as a topic of discussion by Nike in 2017. In 2019 every sneaker released by the Swoosh featured the new label.

When I discuss the shaky ground of authentication it can be summed up in this bit of information from the article quoted at the start of this chapter[15]:

> Recently, Nike's "Air Jordan 1 Retro High OG "Court Purple" and "Air Jordan 1 Retro High OG "Pine Green" also used anti-theft buckles. But Nike's anti-theft buckle is different from all previous sneaker anti-theft buckles. This time, Nike's anti-theft buckle contains RFID tags

---

[15] https://www.nfctagfactory.com/news/Nike-will-introduce-RFID-as-a-new-means-of-after-sales-counterfeit-detection.html

and uses RFID technology... Nike's official website can provide return and exchange services. [Some] Nike customers ... specialize in replacing the genuine shoes they receive with fake goods. Nike lacks effective or quick means of checking the authenticity of products. The official website after-sales personnel are not fully capable of identifying true and false, so the official website to prevent the replacement of fakes is weak.

What exactly is the above quote saying?

StockX, GOAT and Stadium Goods offer authenticity. They have built their brands on the fact that you don't have to worry when you purchase kicks from their businesses. Nike has finally invested in RFID allowing Nike to handle authentication "in-house".

Should RFID be a concern for the parties involved long-term with investments into StockX and GOAT and other platforms?

You would assume my answer would be yes, but it's not so black and white. The concern over authentication based businesses only occurs if those businesses are relying on authentication as the differing factor between "us and them".

Nike has implemented measures to offset the abundance of fake kicks. The strategy for utilizing RFID isn't quite in place but the new size labels allows for the natural progression of RFID to show provenance, much like paperwork for a work of art.

If brands begin doing this, companies utilizing authentication as a means of differentiation will be disrupted. This is important as **traditional retail** begins to prepare for life post COVID-19 they will need to understand what they are up against in the third party e-commerce platforms. Especially if those platforms continue making connections with brands as the **adidas 80s x StockX** launch did.

> *In the instance of our adidas Campus 80s MakerLab IPO, Bids came in from customers across 62 countries and outstripped product supply 10:1.*[16]

Everything that I've written thus far appears to be an attack on StockX. That really isn't the case. The intent thus far is to present both sides of the discussion which can't take place when companies simply access data on sales through retail channels. The analysis needed to create stronger retail can't take place based solely on point of sales data presented to show trending. In order to create smarter

---

[16] https://stockx.com/news/state-of-resale/

businesses the dialogue has to come from within the walls of retails and brands, and that dialogue has to be combined with information from the grey areas. Disruptions happen because advice and input is ignored. Disruptions also take place when those in executive and management positions fail to utilize the members of the team who participate in the day to day functions of the company. COVID-19 has exposed the weakness of the chain of command. The position of CEO means very little if the warehouse worker doesn't walk through the door.

Nike, adidas, New Balance, and all brands have the ability to disrupt resale with the addition of RFID and supply chain monitoring. The closure of businesses during the Coronavirus will expedite the disruption of retail and the disruption of resale. Brands are going to try to regain the lost income. At least brands should be thinking this way. Chances are they aren't.

The irony is resale platforms that haven't made a decision to self-regulate will disrupt themselves. A free market is one thing, but to create a situation where everyone has the same opportunity to sell the same product eventually diminishes the value of that product.

Chapter

8

The Democratization of Sneaker Resale

StockX has democratized the retail process by creating a marketplace that functions autonomously and without checks and balances for the seller or buyer. There is a drawback to the ease in which anyone can utilize StockX. The site has diminished the amount of business savvy that could be generated by learning about the resale business and the sneaker industry. If you have a phone and enough dollars, you can participate in the business of selling sneakers. It doesn't matter that you don't wear kicks, or that you didn't draw sneakers on the cover of your books in high school, or that you bought Puma's because of MC Shan… the history and passion of loving sneakers as a facet of Hip-Hop isn't a requirement for participating in the financial aspects of the sneaker industry.

The democratization of sneaker resale has not been a bonus for the culture or for the business ecosystem for shoe sales. What's happened is that there used to be a time when you were learning every aspect of launching a business when you were selling sneakers.

You had to:

- understand packing and shipping
- learn about customer service
- choose and utilize the right tools to make sure packages reached their destination
- learn about and deal with chargebacks and claims
- learn to write copy and develop plans for marketing
- be capable of warehousing and storing shoes correctly
- make decisions on pricing

Sneaker resale in many ways allowed for an education on the sneaker industry that could prepare a person to open a store and utilize a multifaceted approach to getting kicks to the consumer. You had to know your product.

StockX has changed this and I won't pretend that I'm not benefiting from it. StockX has expedited the ability to sell shoes and made it a much simpler process. In 2005 there weren't any people in Memphis selling sneakers unless they worked with AAU teams and had access to kicks because of players. Actually this isn't true. There was a lady from Kentucky, a guy from Arkansas and me. We had full run of the local stores and could buy without any problems. I wasn't online at the time. I was setting up at the local flea market as the only guy with "real" shoes. I also sold my own shoes under my Sho-Shot brand and then under ARCH.

At any rate I was the only person here buying to flip, which changed around 2009. As this changed over time, the market for sneakers grew. Today the market is cluttered with *Sellers*. I'm sure this is the same with any city. This democratization of sneaker resale is unlike any other industry outside of the luxury resale business. In the luxury business and in the sneaker business there is an amount of fear associated with the purchase of a product from an unauthorized third-party location. Websites like *The Real Real* and *StockX* capitalize on the fear that customers have of receiving a product that's not authentic.

The authentication service allows the business to prosper. However, when anyone can participate in the business creating a level playing field because everything is much simpler and more straightforward, the problem becomes the adjustment to the pricing structure of sneakers.

If you refer to my earlier discussion on the Kyrie 6, you know where I'm heading. MSRP on release day for a shoe is established by the brand; retailers are required to adhere to those MSRP and SRP's. As Nike expanded in the 90's into the 2000's they added more retail locations. This expansion happened on a smaller scale with other brands, but Nike's growth was considerable. The brand didn't stop with adding accounts to wholesale (which they began to pull back on in 2017) Nike opened their own doors as well.

This created a situation where the new (and old) account brick and mortar locations began to compete for the customer via sales and promotions in the 2010s. Both retail and brands began to rely on sales to get the customer in the door. Some brick and mortars began selling kicks early. Employees at mainstream stores began scanning barcodes and inputting sales on the release day. I saw managers get fired for this. These things didn't initially *shape* resale, but as more early releases leaked into the market customers decided they didn't want certain models which lead to the value of sneakers dropping almost immediately after the shoes were released. This did shape retail and it began shaping resale.

Think about it like this, if you walk in a restaurant for pizza and the person ahead of you only pays ten dollars for their pizza when the sign says 15, the next person won't be willing to pay 15 and the baseline for that price is now 10. When the pizzas stop selling at 10 dollars, the store decides to sell the pizzas at 5 each and the price is now set because people realize they can wait and get a better deal. The only way to increase the price again is by improving the product (or service)... This pizza analogy is important for explaining a lot of problems in all industries not just the sneaker business.

When resale began it existed as a means of finding rare or limited release sneakers. I could walk in Nike in 2005 and find Jordans; take those same shoes out to the flea market and barber shops and flip them with ease. When I transitioned to eBay, sneaker resale was still about hard to find kicks, but as Nike increased wholesale accounts, urban accounts like *The Athlete's Foot* were acquired and mergers began to take place. Nike relied heavily on *Futures* and they wanted wholesale accounts. Places on the East Coast that had Nike accounts since the 80s were the original shops where sneaker culture was born. As new accounts began to pop up in small towns in the south in the 2000s the search for kicks expanded. Note: Nike stopped reporting Futures as evidence of growth in 2016 as they moved closer to naming their DTC strategy.

Remember, mom and pops, and small chains were vital in the growth of Nike as a brand. In the 90s and the 2000s there were hidden pockets of small retail shops. These shops held gems. In an attempt to continue to diversify my own inventory I began traveling which meant I couldn't set up at the flea market so I moved heavy into eBay. Around 2009 resale was no longer about hard to find kicks, it became about getting the best deal without leaving the couch. Once people began buying on eBay and then on Amazon, mom and pop shops never transitioned to online sales. They didn't have to, but they did have to contend with more Nike accounts showing up in big cities and small towns. Around 2011 Footlocker began shifting to online sales and actually grew online faster than the brands did. Nike also began investing into Nike.com considerably.

The nature of business is to change. Customers have to be acquired and maintained. A combination of marketing, merchandising and product constantly updated should inspire engagement and purchasing. When there are an abundance of products available, it contributes to a problematic marketplace. Sneakers grew from million dollar companies to billion dollar companies fueled by aspirational products. There are now so many options available it is only natural that sales would crescendo at some point.

Blaming StockX or GOAT for damaging resale/retail is a fallacy. The foundation for sneaker resale began as more accounts were granted by brands. These accounts failed to hire people who actually knew what they were selling and the store experience was based on newness as opposed to education. The consumer began to see that brick and mortar stores held sales and they saw big box warehouse stores getting better product. They also saw sneakers at *off price* stores like *Ross, Marshall's and Kohl's*. Parents became more judicious with their dollars and small accounts began relying on "urban" cash buyers because these are people who simply wanted the coolest pairs. That *cash* moat became a safety net, but the brands around 2014 began to see the growth of online sales as a growth area and as they began implementing strategies they also opened more brand doors themselves. This shift to brand doors meant that smaller accounts were going to suffer. This was good for sneaker resale because there were deals to be made.

Something funny happened along the way… the promotional environment that enabled million dollar resale to take place also reduced the ability for resale to take place from mainstream stores such as Footlocker and Finish Line. A battle began for the best shoes. Relationships became about greased palms, people were fired, connections were lost and then remade and the entire time third party resale online was being shook up by Amazon and encroached upon by the new third party, StockX and GOAT, which was good initially because those channels were about premium sales. Those sites have quickly shifted and a race to the bottom has begun because sneaker resale is now about who can get what the cheapest and quickest.

The democratization of sneaker resale in the third party marketplace is now a war to get to the dollar faster than the next person.

StockX, as an open market place, allows for the bid/price to be set by the consumer and that's great for the consumer. However, when a product can be purchased prior to release or on the day of release below the MSRP of brick-and-mortar stores it creates a situation where money rules the roost; love for the sneaker hunt is abandoned and seasoned resale vets, who can tell you almost anything about the history of kicks, are fighting old White men and old Black men in khakis and button downs with their phones out buying ten pair of Fear of Gods because they saw them first. Those men then return the shoes in a few days because they accepted the lowest offers and the shoes aren't selling anymore.

Does this sound personal? Yep.

Is it StockX's fault? Kinda…

A democracy is a beautiful thing, until you walk into your favorite stores and have to deal with 20 new people standing in front of boxes with their phones out grabbing kicks and then having to take whatever on those kicks because they need the money back to pay bills. A democracy is a beautiful thing until an entire family, mom, dad, grandpa, grandma, and every kid show up, *every day,* to buy every pair of a Jordan 1. A democracy is great, but sometimes the people who own the ship shouldn't allow the crew to have a voice, they need to make executive decisions. These decisions have to be made because the market can no longer correct itself. This should make both brands and retailers worried. When the market can't correct itself it stays trending in the direction of momentum, with small anomalies thrown in.

Just because it's a great time to be a collector because it's easy to find kicks, doesn't mean it's a great time. The sneaker biz is more impersonal and disconnected. Regular stores are paying the price of competing against machines with investment capital who advertise more than any of the brick and mortar accounts can afford to. Because 3rd party sites like StockX can continuously promote, they are reaching pockets of the population I don't think the sites intended. This is diminishing the *per transaction* at retail and online.

Data time: While a micro-set of data isn't reflective of the entire market, all research is done with sample sizes. This information is from my data via StockX. I took the time to breakdown transactions by 100 transactions. For clarity, every 100 pair of shoes I sold, I took the average price of the shoes to reach the transaction price. Earlier in the book I wrote that my average sold price has been falling on StockX since I began using the platform in 2017. For someone else who uses bots to grab ten pair of Travis Scotts or Supreme products, those numbers will not look like this. For someone who has a system in place to acquire sneakers early, their numbers won't look like this. Here are 5 consecutive weeks:

7/12/2019 – 7/19/2019
$102.19/Transaction

7/19/2019 – 7/24/2019
$104.88/Transaction

7/24/2019 – 7/28/2019
$95.87/Transaction

7/28/2019 – 8/1/2019
$91.01/Transaction

8/1/2019 – 8/8/2019
$87.01/Transaction

In Chapters 1 & 2 I explained that my average per transaction had decreased. I did so to introduce the idea of self-regulation to correct the market. I don't expect StockX to regulate itself. I don't expect brands to stop overproducing sneakers. I don't expect retail stores who already have accounts to care about creating better in-store experiences and I don't expect them to care about content creation and taking on the qualities of a media company. I may have focused this on StockX, but that is because any research requires a control. This book at its heart is about new businesses and entrepreneurs entering a moment in retail history unlike anything MBA programs and experienced workers in this industry have ever seen.

Note (added during editing on 5-12-2020):

As I edited this book StockX launched an IPO with New Balance and Los Angeles based brand No Vacancy. The IPO report was posted on 5/12/2020. No other sneaker sites or business sites discussed the event. Like the *adidas Campus 80s IPO* it went unnoticed outside of the sneaker culture niche.

The IPO confirmed my thoughts on StockX as a valuable platform. Authentication no longer needs to be the selling point of the website. The *adidas Campus 80s IPO* was research. The *New Balance IPO* was confirmation. The New Balance IPO garnered the site's best performance in an IPO. Could this have happened because of the quarantine? Possibly, but at a time when the site was facing backlash over their own issues with COVID-19, they launched an IPO that could have sold 14,000 pair in a three day window. Sales through the platform haven't slowed as states have begun to reopen. The stats from the latest IPO are both exciting and problematic.

> *After four days of action on the StockX marketplace, the New Balance 650 x No Vacancy Inn IPO garnered nearly 14,000 unique Bids, the highest number of Bids in any StockX IPO to date. It was also a truly global release: 30% of Bids originated outside of the United States, and 61 different countries and territories around the world were represented. Across all sizes, the average clearing price was a whopping $415. For individual sizes, the clearing prices ranged from a low of $325 (for size 7.5) to a high of $500 (for size 12). This was the highest clearing price in StockX IPO history.[17]*

The importance of studying the StockX platform at this point should be clear.

I hate to utilize an overused rap lyric, but it's time to reintroduce this book to you because I'm about to do what businesses have to do. I'm about to shift and look at why remerging from COVID-19, or from bankruptcy, or launching as a startup is so difficult.

---

[17] https://stockx.com/news/new-balance-no-vacancy-inn-ipo-recap/

Chapter

9 Reintroduction

The store has become a showroom that can no longer convert the consumer based on value alone. Retail has shifted and stores are no longer capable of existing as warehouses storing products for brands. Today, the customer will walk in, try on the product (or pick it up, depending on the business) and will then order it online. This **showroom aspect** *(a term that took on this meaning after speaking with Greg Garber a manager of a retail sneaker store)* is generating a new issue at retail.

If a product is not in stock, the immediate job of sales leads and managers is to move the customer to digital. The job used to be to earn the sale on the floor. Now associates have to capture sales via digital channels in store. This has been labeled as omni-channel. Systems like Retail-Pro allow for warehouse and online integration, but the cost is high for a startup or a small business. The cost for not utilizing a system like this is even higher as many restaurants and retailers have learned during the COVID-19 crisis.

As the brands become more active, retailers are in the precarious position of not only fighting other chains for the consumer dollar; they are also fighting the brands they carry. This has pushed the traditional retail model towards a breaking point, especially big box stores who have yet to understand that they are not *stores* anymore. Both retail outlets and brands have to consider themselves as media companies engaging the consumer in the digital space and in the physical location. The store is both showroom and in-store purchasing option. The store is also a warehouse and fulfillment center. Finally, the store has to become an experiential, interactive activation through digital and brick and mortar merchandising.

An interactive concept has to begin with a design that is aesthetically appealing which inspires digital responses. When I enter your store I should want to Instagram my visit. I should also be able to see the product in action. PERCH, iPads or monitors are perfect for moving the CX from online to in-store.

- There is a reason the *makeup/beauty* product channel is one of the fastest growing segments in retail.
- There is a reason that a *brand* store **can** function in the old way of warehousing.
- There is a reason malls are seeing the loss of anchor stores; and long-time luxury stores like Barneys are suffering as smaller digitally created brands like Warby Parker, GREATS Brand, Allbirds are shifting to brick and mortar.

Small is more cost effective and allows for speed and responsiveness. If big box stores don't elevate the consumer experience, then they die.

Restructuring, or starting a business, begins with a more user friendly and informative online experience that transitions to in-store merchandising, all catering to the customer experience. Retail brick and mortar can't funnel without a purpose. Floor layouts are just as vital as cash wrap. *Dope* product and cash customers are no longer a moat for urban stores, and luxury is no longer a driver of foot traffic at the high end. A retailer has to inspire loyalty and engagement.

Large luxury stores like Nordstrom's, Dillard's and Macy's now carry *stores inside of stores*, to capture new markets. Large stores have a unique opportunity to offset leasing issues hindering profit by breaking themselves up, but this can only work if the customer experience is elevated.

Brands can no longer create vast SKUs as smaller more agile brands are creating more expensive, but longer lasting, eco-friendly options. Why sell twenty 10 dollar tees when you can sell five 40 dollar environmentally conscious, well designed tees?

Retail merchandising has shifted. Store design has to be about sight-lines, loss prevention, and flow, just as much as it is about *Instagram and Snapchat*. In old school traditional retail the salesperson was a teacher on the floor; this subsided as retail became about warehousing in the 80s and 90s.

Today, digital has forced the salesperson to be a tech guru with a depth of knowledge about the product that is on par with a consumer who is more informed than any other time in the history of retail.

This section of the book will build on the previous segment, but the goal is to create ideas that make you feel that you are actively participating in this discussion. I want you to consider every moment of the retail experience. Here are a few things to consider while reading and for when you begin to plan your launch or relaunch strategy:

1. When you walk into a store take note of what is placed where and how it is presented (merchandising and marketing).
2. Look at how brands are positioned in the store.
3. Look at if the store is compartmentalized effectively and then check brand websites (products carried in stores) for new marketing strategies or concepts to see how they can inform strategies in store (If the Nike website is promoting a new campaign, is that campaign being conveyed in retail doors?).

Retailers and entrepreneurs are returning to a world shaped by the dominant brands in their industries. To stay on topic, the sneaker industry is being shaped by Nike. Nike has forced every brand to expand beyond athleisure back into performance. Think about the businesses that went bankrupt and are returning or preparing to relaunch: Payless, Sheikh, The Sports Authority and Modells. These stores, except The Sports Authority, are in/returning into a market where off priced retail is a competitor. I can walk into Kohl's, Ross, and Marshall's and purchase Nike, adidas, and Kenneth Cole footwear. I can walk from the footwear area of these off-price retailers and purchase matching apparel, all for the price of 60.00 dollars or less.

As I said earlier, new businesses and reemerging businesses are competing with traditional accounts, off-priced retail and the brand. Even if a customer can walk into Kohls and buy all they need, they will still *showroom* at that location just as much as they will showroom at Foot Locker.

To be honest, there are too many options available, but these stores are not going to willingly close; which means that in every industry businesses all have to understand the rise of direct-to-consumer strategies by brands. Take for instance a brand like Under Armour who invested heavily in Kohl's as a partner less than five years ago. As a part of their restructuring plan, they are paring down those relationships to regain control of their *perception*.

Stores like, Nordstrom's Rack, Sacks Off 5th, that have long been places where young professionals could buy a cost effective pair of business shoes, and stores like Target, Wal-Mart, even a place like Payless (emerging from bankruptcy in North America), where parents could buy shoes for their children, all have to account for one fact: Cost is no longer a driver of engagement in the same way it was in 2015. Retail outlets have created their own clearance stores and Brands have followed suit. Young professionals are becoming more savvy and eco-conscious and parents are aware of all of the options available to them.

Stores like Payless and Modell's once had the cash customer as a moat, but as I discussed in my previous book, the cash customer is transitioning into the digital marketplace at a much faster rate than at any other time. CashApp and PayPal have allowed the cash customer to have a banking system as opposed to relying solely on check cashing businesses. Smart phone access, third party apps, Instagram's culture of cool are all factors in buying decisions for cash customers today.

How does an entrepreneur take all of this information and create a company? How do companies previously built on cost compete when the entire retail industry is promotion driven? How do businesses reenter this landscape?

This reintroduction once again is mimicking business; it's changing directions. StockX may have allowed me to establish how third party marketplaces have changed retail, but there is a need for analysis and solutions, not just the delivery of data telling the industry what is, or is not selling. In the following chapters, the goal is to provide a discussion that becomes a catalyst for conversation allowing for a smarter launch or reentry.

Chapter

10

Remember, Sneaker Culture is Mainstream

The parents and people who shopped at The Sports Authority, Payless, and Modell's were not sneakerheads and probably had very little understanding of sneaker culture. This has changed in the last ten years. Everyone in the United States has been introduced to sneaker collecting via documentaries and due to the influx of investments taking place in the industry. The number of small and big businesses that have grown out of sneaker culture has spawned branches catering to the market.

Sneaker retail outlets that have gone bankrupt and are going bankrupt thrived at a time when high fashion wasn't interested in sneakers. In the past you would never see sneakers on the catwalks in Paris. Now fashion houses like LVMH, are hiring sneaker and streetwear designers to head their companies. Those same fashion houses are investing in resale platforms like Stadium Goods.

Nike has collaborated with Dior and Vogue. There are brand partnerships with sneaker influencers and small retail outlets like New Orleans based sneaker shop Sneaker Politics making a shoe with Saucony based on beignets from Café Du Monde.

Motivational speakers and business owners are telling everyday people to invest in sneakers the way they invest in stocks. A recent book by Dylan Dittrich named *Sneakonomic Growth: Scarcity, Storytelling, and the Arrival of Sneakers as an Asset Class*, looks at sneakers as assets in a similar fashion to long term investments like mutual funds or stocks.

Parents are no longer able to buy their kids a cheap pair of kicks. Parents are listening to their children who are using Snapchat and Instagram and those kids can tell you every Jordan retro, so they don't want to wear shoes that aren't cool.

The rise of social media has contributed to extensive bullying for kids and young adults. Now more than ever your clothing is your calling card.

Is that right?

Of course it isn't. Should parents cater to children and buy them what's cool in an attempt to avoid bullying? I think so, but the shoes shouldn't define the kid. The reality is that sneakers provide cache amongst peers.

A new or reemerging company, right now, might have an opportunity to claim a small share of the market with low-end products in the international market with casual and athletic footwear. This is changing rapidly as brands open doors internationally.

In the North American market this simply isn't the case anymore. Consider that the successful startups that have launched in the last five years, Allbirds, Greats and a recent startup in COMUNITYmade footwear are all catering to a consumer who understands the value of what they are buying. These brands born online moved into physical retail not with an inexpensive product, they all created footwear that was sustainable and made with quality materials.

I attempted to enter the market with an inexpensive model that didn't utilize premium materials. I didn't focus on sustainability or quality, just cost and I failed. The only company capable of jumping in the water and making inexpensive footwear seems to be Amazon. As Payless went bankrupt Amazon launched several footwear companies. This moves me too far ahead.

Sneaker Culture is Mainstream. Soccer moms who have three pairs call themselves sneakerheads. The demographic that created sneaker culture is now entering their fifties and 55 year old men care more about their shoes than twenty-somethings. This shift creates a complex marketplace for startups and reemerging businesses.

Price can no longer drive engagement as brands have made a conscious decision to drive sales direct-to-consumer. In taking a more direct approach wholesale relationships have fractured and bankruptcies and store closures are taking place from big box sporting goods stores, to neighborhood cheap shoe outlets. It's a known fact that traditional retail big box stores like Dillard's and Macy's are also facing serious headwinds.

Nike has opened over 300 brick and mortar locations in the last six years placing many of their stores in direct competition with their own accounts. What this has contributed to is Nike being able to reach the consumer who once shopped at discount outlets like Payless and middle income stores like Modell's. Nike is even hitting urban accounts and 'family' stores.

The Nike Clearance Store, for example, caters to the urban/cash consumer and the Nike Factory Store caters to low to middle income families. Statista[18] shows that in **2009**:

- Nike had 140 stores and
- Converse (owned by Nike) had 43 stores.

In **2019**

- Nike had 217 stores and
- Converse had 109 stores.

---

[18] https://www.statista.com/statistics/241642/number-of-nike-stores-in-the-us-since-2008/

In these stores Nike has made an effort to enroll all visitors into their Nike.com and SNKRS digital platforms. At these doors the Swoosh also has the ability to provide deep discounts on their footwear. Is there a correlation between the increase in Nike stores and the bankruptcy of The Sports Authority and Payless, two chains at different ends of the spectrum?

Payless was a place where a customer could drop in and grab a pair of shoes for all of their kids at 20 dollars a pair. Nike now offers "cool" footwear at a similar pricing structure allowing kids and adults to become a part of the culture of cool at the same price. The Sports Authority had baseball bats, soccer balls, backpacks, all types of sports gear and training essentials… Nike Clearance Stores carry all of those items.

Pinning this on Nike solely is not fair. Remember I said that retailers entering this market are doing so at a dangerous moment? Kohl's had 637 stores in 2004[19] by 2013 they had 1,158 stores. Last year in 2019 they partnered with Amazon for returns[20]. Kohl's began

---

[19] https://www.referenceforbusiness.com/history2/15/Kohl-s-Corporation.html
[20] https://www.kohls.com/feature/amazon.jsp

as an off-price retailer for the middle class, it has since expanded and has become popular with all demographics. The same can be said of the TJX chains, home of Marshalls. As always I frame the discussion around sneakers, but if you're reading this book and you aren't in the sneaker industry, remember... Marshalls, TJ Maxx, Kohls, Ross, carry everything that Sears carried except outdoor equipment and car parts. What happened to Sears? I reference Nike because it gives a baseline for the discussion, and I visit Nike stores more than any other retail outlet. This is a discussion I hope will cross over into other categories.

On a recent informal trip to a Nike Clearance Store during tax time I ran into the Manager, District Manager and RVP of Finish Line in the Memphis area. They visited because they wanted to see what the traffic was like at the store. When they walked in, the line at the Nike store was about 40 people deep and every register was open. Customers were on their phones using Facetime to talk with those at home to check which pair of shoes they wanted. Nike was having a 30% off sale. They offer these sales consistently. Sometimes the sales are 20% off. I made a purchase of 4 pair of shoes. As a military veteran I get an additional 10% off. This is what I purchased:

Nike Special Forces Air Force 1 – SRP: 180.00 Discounted Price 29.99 with an additional 30% off = 20.00.

Nike DayBreak SP – SRP: 100.00 Discounted Price 59.99 with an additional 30% off = 31.00.

Air Jordan 3 Retro OG True Blue – SRP 220.00 Discounted Price 149.99 with an additional 30% off = 105.99

    I purchased 2 pair of the Air Jordan 3 Retro. My total price for this purchase was 269.61. All of these shoes I sold on StockX for a gross of 387.13 as I stood in the store talking to the store manager because he wanted to see how the process worked and I wanted to prove a point. I don't know how the conversation between the store manager of Finish Line and his bosses went, but I'm sure he gave them a clear understanding of the market as it relates to resale and why the Nike Store was flushed with people while Finish Line's flagship store in the best mall in the city wasn't crowded at all.

    The customers at the Clearance Store were a mixture of every demographic and class. They all used their phones to look online at reviews and information. Kids throughout the stores talked about being *IG fresh* or *Snapchat fresh*. Kids did the "Shoot" dance for TikTok and this atmosphere is a daily occurrence. Parents realize what happens at school and they aren't so quick to buy their kids a pair of "cheap" shoes.

Since The Sports Authority went bankrupt and Payless closed 600+ stores in 2017 the entire market has shifted. Sneaker Culture made brands carried in Payless "hot" again. Champion is considered a legacy brand and now sells at FootLocker and has a *high end* collaboration with Casbia Footwear with shoes that cost 300.00 dollars.

What does all of this mean for startups and reemerging businesses?

Sneaker Culture is no longer niche. Everyone wants to be "cool" and Nike's Consumer Direct Offense has altered the landscape for all athletic retailers. Stores can't win with cheap shoes because adidas, Under Armour, Puma and Nike utilize off-price retail for takedown models of their footwear and apparel. Nike uses its own store system for their returns and overstock from Nike digital. The urban customers who are shopping at the Clearance Store are also visiting Marshalls. The family shoppers are able to pick up name brand gear at Kohl's and Ross.

It's not just Nike or off-price retailers that pose a threat, it's stores like Shoe Warehouse or DSW from groups like Designer Brands and Affiliated Brands. DSW is taking a page from athletic companies and fashion brands by realizing the power of influencers. As bankruptcies have hit footwear companies, DSW made adjustments in business and casual footwear by working with entertainers like J-Lo. The DSWs of the world understand that selling to the customer today requires creating an experience and the creation of private labels within the chain. As I've mentioned over and over, *to compete with the vendor will require becoming the vendor.*

New retail outlets and old, entrepreneurs and bigger startups are going to be pressed from every angle as everyone emerges from the COVID-19 crisis. Even if the coronavirus hadn't disrupted everything, these obstacles were already here.

This doesn't mean that you should be discouraged if you are making the decision to launch your idea. Even if you are a company that has had to restructure, like Sheikh has, if you walk into the room with the knowledge of what you're up against you increase the likelihood of success. Take a moment and do the research on businesses that began during depressions or economic downturns. What you'll find is that there is opportunity in the most difficult moments. Just because you have to fight an established, bigger business it doesn't mean you should pack it up before you start.

Chapter

11

The Time is Now for Private Label and Startups

At this point it's probably clear that all industries are adjusting to this new *golden wave* provided by the internet. In the 90s there was a *dot com* boom... and collapse. Today, because of crowdfunding, people with great ideas can find funding. The internet has also increased the ease at which you can connect to factories in Europe and Asia if you want to produce a product. COVID-19 has shown the fragility in the supply chain for importing, but that doesn't mean a startup is without a way to manufacture here in the U.S.

Ten years ago footwear companies were not as plentiful. Since 2010 the list of DTC brands has grown in North America and abroad. Here are the names of a few new sneaker brands:

- Greats Brand 2014
- Allbirds 2014
- Clearweather 2014
- NOBULL 2015
- York Athletics 2016
- Cortica (UK)
- Sonra (Germany 2016)
- COMUNITYmade 2017
- Society Nine 2017

One company I didn't mention above was born when a former designer who worked with Nike and with Yeezy made a decision to step away from the corporate world and launch his own business platform. Jeff Henderson is the founder of a triple threat collective:

- **AndThem** is the creative agency.
- **GoodThin.gs** is the social impact driver.
- **NinetyNine Products** is the in-house brand.

This book exists to explain stories like this. Jeff's collection of platforms is a reason why other startups and businesses reentering the market is complicated.

For the sake of brevity and instead of spending an inordinate amount of time explaining every aspect of Jeff Henderson's idea, I will focus primarily on NinetyNine Products. NinetyNine is not in direct competition with all of the other brands listed above. They aren't very big. Greats and Allbirds have both garnered million and billion dollar valuations. But, 99 is an example of the creative expansion taking place in the footwear industry. This same expansion is happening in other industries. Just as the established big companies are disrupting wholesale by going DTC, and third party tech sites are disrupting retail accounts, startups are returning the favor and taking small shares away from the giants. Whittling away at the giant oaks and those carvings are very noticeable.

These alternatives to Nike, adidas, Under Armour and New Balance are primarily creating casual shoes as opposed to athletic footwear, except NOBULL, Society Nine, York Athletics and NinetyNine. The first three companies are aiming squarely at the performance market. They are smart enough to realize they can't compete in traditional sports, so they are taking on the niche sports of Crossfit and MMA/Boxing. Each company has found its own path and while many haven't heard of the brands, they have been able to create small pockets of fans. The other companies listed above, Sonra and COMUNITYmade in particular, are making 'athleisure' footwear that is handcrafted and made in limited product runs. Sonra is intriguing because it was founded by one of the former owners of the extremely influential Solebox Sneaker Shop, Hikmet Sugoer. Hikmet has collaborations with a range of big brands. He took his work there and created Sonra. Sonra initially made a retro running inspired sneaker named the Sonra Proto. He has expanded the lineup, but he is well known as a person who dislikes resellers who don't respect the culture around sneakers. The irony is his limited footwear that people outside of the sneaker world have probably never heard of, resales for twice as much as his SRP.

As I said, I'll focus on NinetyNine for a moment because of how they have taken the process of building collections in a uniquely different direction. The most important aspect for 99 is how they decide their designs.

Henderson established his brand in a way that is in complete contrast to bigger brands. His first sneaker launch, The Point, was designed with educators in mind. It's a performance model that amazingly features a full length carbon plate, but upon first noticing the model it looks like a chunky soled casual model. The shoe rings in at under 100 dollars, while Nike's 4% Vapor with a full carbon plate rings up at $250.00 plus. That accomplishment for a startup is pretty important stuff, but again the why behind the design choice is the most important aspect.

With NinetyNine each release becomes a calling card for celebrating the unsung heroes in various job positions. NinetyNine's The Point, with colorway names like *Chalk and Whiteboard,* is a shoe donated to teachers in New York. The marketing arm, *And Them*, isn't dedicated to promoting the brand. The marketing for NinetyNine celebrates other small companies. This selflessness, as the company grows, will endear the brand to fans of the products.

The old model of cheap and accessible, I have to repeat, isn't going to drive the connection to the consumer anymore. Throughout the various categories of footwear there is now an option for every demographic. Allbirds developed a wool shoe with a sugar based outsole technology named SweetFoam:

> *It's so self-sufficient, in fact, that when it's processed, its biomass is extracted to literally power the mill and fertilize the next year's crop. When we transform it into our SweetFoam™ shoe sole, it contours to your feet for bouncy comfort that lets you let loose.*[21]

Allbirds launched as a fitness company and understood something I didn't; eco-friendly products will inspire connection to the potential consumer. This garnered the brand a billion dollar valuation. The company only carries 5 SKUs on the men's and women's side. The shoes ring up at 95 -135 dollars. A price that is much more than Nike, adidas and bigger brands' entry level products. The footwear is both casual and business ready. Young professionals love the sustain-

---

[21] https://www.allbirds.com/pages/our-materials-sugar

ability narrative around the company and this has allowed Allbirds to reach a different consumer than when they originally launched via Kickstarter as the brand 3 over 7.

Allbirds was made possible because of crowdfunding. I ran a Kickstarter in 2014 and since 2014 the number of footwear companies launched via Crowdfunding has grown considerably. Former designer at Under Armour and PENSOLE graduate Matt Walters created his boot company CODDI in 2019. Inkkas launched via Kickstarter and was invested into by Marcus Lemonis of the television show *The Profit*. There are fashion brands which have been born on Kickstarter and Indiegogo and all of these companies gain the benefit of being supported by individuals who saw value in the story they created.

Crowdfunding born brands aren't foolproof, but they show evidence of the shift in consumerism. Buyers want to be delivered a story and in order to compete in today's market, startups and entrepreneurs will have to be cost effective, eco-friendly and capable of developing a consistent discussion around technology proprietary to the brand. If there isn't technology then the company has to have a mission.

COMUNITYmade's "Founders are veterans of the footwear industry having led Asics marketing and Toms' creative direction."[22] The company wanted to build a business that returned manufacturing to the United States. They also wanted to serve their community. Every pair, similar to Toms, contributes money to non-profits or charity based organizations. This company creates footwear with a premium price point, but their model connects because they use local cobblers to create their handmade footwear.

Each of the companies above are clearly not in the same realm as the retailers reemerging from bankruptcy like Payless, and they are definitely not like Modell's who is entering bankruptcy, but when you consider the stories around each brand and why they were created and then you add the fact that retailers like DSW are providing cost effective footwear connected to major influencers, every demographic has a brand/retailer that speaks to them.

What will new companies do to speak to the consumer? Will price continue to be the strategy companies build their foundation up-

---

[22] https://www.linkedin.com/company/comunity-made/about/

on? I already failed with that strategy so let my story be a cautionary tale. Modell's did everything correctly as a retailer. They built a robust in-store ordering system, but the company was still caught in the wave of DTC by brands. Sheikh was an urban account that thought it had the protection of the cash customer, but the cash customer is no longer a *Captain America* sized shield. As a matter of fact it's not a shield at all. It's simply a small speed bump on the road to cash customers becoming a part of the digital society. Payless used brands like Champion and Pro Wings to mimic popular designs of bigger brands, but now Champion is considered a heritage brand and carried in Foot Locker and making high end collabs.

How will startups counter wholesale accounts in urban communities like City Gear or DTLR where they have been given the green light to hold *Buy 1 Get One Half Off* sales on adidas, Puma, New Balance and other brands?

Can a new wholesale based retail business be cost effective, athletic, business and casual while also delivering storytelling that helps their customers be better athletes and entrepreneurs?

On my site I have written about 30 new footwear companies. I've only listed a few in this chapter, but it's clear this current market is not the footwear arena that allowed different companies to exist for so many years before bankruptcy. In the international market Under Armour, adidas, Nike and Puma are opening more doors; which will chip away at opportunities in the international market for startup retail and brands, but that shouldn't frustrate a person diving into small business.

Sonra and Cortica are both brands born in Europe, one at the premium price point, the other at the low end. oth. *off the hook* is a brand launched in 2017 in Paris. COVID-19 has hit that business extremely hard, but their decision to utilize handmade sneakers built with upcycled tire tread is evidence that this is a different day.

Everyday a new company rises from the digital arena and as they gain ground they move into brick and mortar. All brands are dealing with an informed, but distracted consumer. How do prospective retailers attract the different demographics, in particular the groups I think offer the most opportunity, parents and professionals?

Chapter

12

Parents and Professionals = Forrest and Bubba

First there was Forrest and Jenny. Then there was Forrest and Bubba. Forrest and Jenny gave us Forrest Jr., but Forrest and Bubba gave us camaraderie and a business that transitioned from a fictional book, into a movie and then into an actual brick and mortar restaurant in the real world. Both of Forrest's relationships were born in difficult moments. Jenny eventually died of an unknown disease giving Forrest only a short amount of her life. Bubba died in Forrest's arms during the Vietnam War. The fictional story of a simple man is grounded in the relationships he happened upon.

The COVID-19 quarantine has created a moment where unfortunate circumstances will create businesses. The businesses born during this time will more than likely survive a downturn later, if the person launching the business is working to solve a problem. Is this idealistic thinking? Yes and no.

Forrest Gump is a character who was born in difficult circumstances and tumultuous times; but due to his ability to focus solely on the task at hand he was able to make diamonds from dirt. While his actions were the result of goodness and a childlike belief in right, startups can't be as aloof, but should definitely approach launching a business with attention to how they treat parents and professionals.

Look at that transition! Actually don't look at it, it's kind of rough. What's this allusion to Forrest Gump all about? A difficult start, filled with love, hope and an understanding of the importance of how hard work can contribute to a life filled with meaningful moments and opportunities, but it will take some luck as well. Above all, when you have a little luck and great relationships things become easier. A venture becomes even easier when you know where the target is. Forrest Gump may be a fictitious character, but with the memory and guidance of his friend, he stuck it out in the Gulf during a hurricane when everyone else gave up and Bubba Gump was born.

As stores like Payless and The Sports Authority shuttered, the growth of Amazon continued, online e-commerce/DTC from brands increased and *off price retail* became a warehouse for premium brands, and for classic retailers *off price* became a safe haven. The customers who utilized the different forms of retail range from young people to grandparents. Two demographics are the most important.

To make the references to Forrest Gump more clear, parents were once the life blood of Payless and The Sports Authority, but this demographic has more options in a continuously promotional environment which makes for a complex reentry from bankruptcy. Parents in today's climate are more aware of options in shopping for footwear and apparel for both the household and for employment. In the sneaker industry the number of new businesses could be seen as a problem, but one thing remains true, if a business is armed with the correct information, and that business has a laser focus on two demographics, parents and professionals, that business can find a way to survive in the face of adversity. Did I need an allusion to Forrest Gump to write this last paragraph? Nah, but I enjoyed writing it.

Parents

Footwear purchases (feel free to exchange any business product for footwear) have always been factored into household expenses. Back to School, holidays and tax time were previously guaranteed growth periods for companies in the footwear industry. This is still the case, but brick and mortar accounts have seen consistent declines as brands have taken to offering incentives for shopping in the digital platform systems of their businesses. Opposing retailers have also created loyalty programs that provide coupons and discounts, which helped to move customers of brick and mortar stores away from traditional retail.

One of the most important factors for households considering footwear purchases is the creation of private label by behemoth Amazon. Since 2017 Amazon Prime memberships have increased from 67% to 82% according to Statista and Forbes. Why is this important? Startups, entrepreneurs and businesses returning after COVID-19 or launching for the first time, as I've said countless times throughout this book, are up against a host of competition. Almost everyone in the country has an Amazon Prime account.

Amazon has launched their logistics division and as the company becomes a delivery option they have also built pickup locations throughout every demographic. When this is combined with the fact that low-income consumers are no longer *unbanked/underbanked* and are increasingly participating in the digital economy, Amazon is now the competitor to any business model built on 'cheap' products. Only six years ago Amazon was simply a gateway in footwear with third party sellers on Seller Central, and Zappos as the only footwear company it owned. Zappos is basically a third party vendor on steroids. Zappos once worked with Melissa Rivers, but the company doesn't own a private label[23].

The amount of data and information Amazon compiled from Zappos, the companies who have brand registries and 3rd parties selling through the Seller Central platform allowed the giant to launch Amazon Essentials in Fashion. Under Amazon Essentials, a search of the site using the keywords *'Amazon Essentials Womens Shoes'*

---

[23] https://sgbonline.com/zappos-partners-melissa-rivers-for-private-label-brand/

brings back over 18 styles with a number of their models, like the Mocassin Flat, ranked as the #1 seller in the category[24].

On the Men's side of Amazon Essentials the company has 206 Collective and Urban Shoes Co[25]. In choosing to look at footwear and sportswear businesses that went bankrupt, there is an irony in analyzing one company in particular: Payless.

(This was edited in May 2020 prior to Payless relaunching in North America. As this book ages this section will be a reference for how Payless' website was being operated during their restructuring.)

Introducing a discussion on Amazon as a disruptor for the relaunch of Payless, allows for an analysis of website strategies on reemerging businesses. This is important because Modell's is a model for a brand/retailer that has the ability to enter bankruptcy and come out a different company and Payless allows for the analysis of a company that has completed bankruptcy and is in relaunching mode.

---

[24] https://www.amazon.com/Amazon-Essentials-Leather-Moccasin-Slip

[25] https://www.modernfellows.com/here-are-the-differences-between-amazon-essentials-goodthreads-buttoned-down-and-other-amazon-prime-brands/

Right now Payless is preparing to move from bankruptcy to rebuilding their U.S. market. The international stores for the company remained open and unaffected by the U.S. bankruptcy. The company, as of March 2020, is forwarding their traffic from their online website, which is still active, to Amazon utilizing an affiliate model. For a company reemerging, the Payless website should be making an effort to build a robust digital platform on the current homepage.

There isn't an e-mail capture or newsletter sign-up on their homepage and there isn't information or a blog available for the company to begin discussing strategy and brands the company will carry. Before Payless signs a lease to begin opening stores again, the consumer should be well informed of why they should even take the time to look at Payless as opposed to Amazon or Belk and other retailers.

Professionals

There is an obvious reason I'm focused on two demographics. I've already discussed how Nike's growth in direct-to-consumer is a disruption; but this doesn't speak towards working parents and low income parents who are also professionals. One of the more prominent memories I have of my mom was her tendency to visit a store like Payless and grab a pair of flats for work. When I grew up, and was a basketball coach I remember parents who would visit *The Sports Authority* to find cheap shoes for their young athletes. When I was coaching I eventually took that burden off of the parents by fundraising and buying team shoes.

My mom was a young professional. I may not have seen her that way when my sister and I were kids, but I now realize my mother was trying to create a life and take care of her children. She didn't have a lot of money to spend. Today, Young Professionals, who might not have kids, but have huge student loan debt, who would have once utilized a Payless for footwear are now given the option of loyalty programs with off-retail chain outlets.

Consider Nordstrom's and their Nordy Club Rewards Program and their off price business *Nordstrom's Rack*, and look at how Sacks opened their off-price retail *Sacks Off 5th* and you see reasons for why a business like Payless began to have the problems which led to bankruptcy. Stores like Sacks Off 5th and Nordstrom's Rack offer a big box styled experience that requires consumers to search for savings, but in those stores customers can find Cole Haan business footwear at a fraction of the cost, as well as apparel. Parents and Professionals are two demographics who are constantly looking for bargains and they are always shopping either for their families or for themselves.

What does this mean for a new business trying to avoid the fate of retailers who have been caught in the undertow of the various competitors in the footwear industry?

These startups have to understand that success doesn't arrive via the ease of utilizing Amazon as a platform. I speak with stores right now who use Amazon as their delivery system instead of building their own sites and working hard to create an experience that moves from brick and mortar to online.

This is a caveat section.

Payless is currently forwarding the new traffic for their company to Amazon. The Payless site is still getting 204,000 visits a month, down from the millions per week the site attracted when it was active. That's 204,000 potential customers being funneled to a competitor.

Amazon Essentials is a major problem that should be discussed in as much detail as I've given time to StockX in this book and Nike in my previous work. The brand of Payless was never really recognized as an athletic company. The space Payless occupied was casual and business. Just as Amazon places Payless in a difficult position in business footwear for parents and professionals, Payless finds itself in the same position in athletic footwear fighting a direct-to-consumer focused Nike and other brands. That same difficult position exists in casual footwear with startups and digitally native companies focusing on the environment and on customer service as an option.

The reemergence of Payless has challenges at every angle and throughout all demographics. If this were a Boston Matrix based paper that looked at strengths and weaknesses and I had to deliver my thoughts on whether Payless could reenter with a similar strategy to what they originally had and still have with stores in the international market, I would say that the company shouldn't bother with relaunching especially since they are already giving away their power for the few dollars being generated via Amazon Associates affiliate links.

The reality is Payless has an opportunity to recreate itself if the company is clear on how the various demographics, it once catered to, have been empowered through technology. Modell's will have an opportunity to recreate itself. Sheikh hasn't adjusted and still retains the same model, which is problematic; but if you're a sole proprietor or small business walking into the ocean you have a chance to survive a riptide; if you realize a riptide can happen at any moment.

Chapter 13

The Cash Customer is Finally Digital

Why would I spend one hundred pages discussing how to disrupt something that has earned me 1.5 million dollars in two years? I'm often asked on YouTube where do I buy all of the shoes I sell. When I'm out visiting different stores I'm asked, "How do you do what you do?" In my last book I explained that I tried to build teams. I wanted a sneaker version of Wu-Tang. It never happened. When I realized that it was difficult to build a team the right way in a business that was in many ways worse than the drug game in *Snowfall* or on *Breaking Bad*, I made a decision to shut down and not give information away. I isolated myself. The result was bankruptcy.

I was *The Sports Authority, Payless and Modell's* on a much smaller scale, but I lost everything. I began writing and talking the way I do now because after experiencing the collapse of a business on two different occasions I understood that not sharing meant that I wasn't building. If you aren't building you're destroying. That destruction happens both externally and internally.

I write this because the thousands of books that are out there aren't written from a perspective that is straightforward. When I write that startups, entrepreneurs and businesses launching and reemerging from difficult circumstances should be aware of the new market, I want it to be clear. While I can't reach everyone, someone may read this and avoid the bottom.

There is something very interesting about being at the bottom without any money or credit. You have to become more ingenious. You learn how to manage your money better so you can have more of it and you can get the things that you need and the things you enjoy. I write all of this to say that living in the world of the unbanked and underbanked after being on the other side, gives you a much clearer image of how quickly things change in the financial sector. When middle to high income families learn about new investment opportunities and better ways of shopping or earning, the concept of information trickling down doesn't happen. Information tends to remain in its class. Income inequality remains an issue in politics and in social circles, but more so in life.

A person who is in a low income situation isn't privy to the same data and content as a person in a different income bracket. That doesn't mean information isn't being shared at the lower end of the spectrum. Low income families are always looking for a better way to live, but without information that demographic will continue to do what they've been taught. Get a check, cash it, buy groceries, pay bills and then get things that make you feel better. This demographic learns from their peers, like all demographics learn (not including those who attend institutions of learning).

Unlike me, when I was doing very well and decided to hold on to the information, when people find a way to make their lives a bit easier they share.

How does this introduction relate to this book?

Consumer behavior is a field of study that is critical when planning the launch of a business. In footwear, particularly sneakers, the unbanked and underbanked have long been a safety net for urban retail. I mentioned this in my previous book, but I have to reiterate that businesses starting out today have the benefit of a new segment of consumers.

I've mentioned the crumbling walls of the kingdoms surrounded by what was once *cash customer moats,* in an earlier section. As foot traffic has diminished at urban accounts the question is 'where are the customers shopping'?

This section will not be easy to read, but it is required. Outside of local dopeboys and those who haven't moved away from check cashing businesses as banks, the low-income consumer is slowly moving from unbanked to digital finance companies.

Having written about the transition to digital in my previous book on the sneaker industry, I don't want to dwell on it very long. The previous book was written to tell businesses to become more focused on content and to become like media companies.

This book is being written to tell individuals and businesses to understand the various competitors. To do this it's best if I create a thesis based on something I discussed while talking about StockX. In the earlier chapters I stated that StockX has created a race to the bottom by resellers and this has inadvertently led to a race to the bottom by brands and retailers.

If there is a race to the bottom, the three retailers I've referred to in regard to bankruptcy the most, The Sports Authority, Payless and Modell's should be addressed. Payless was the business focused on inexpensive footwear as their sales strategy. Let's begin there.

I attempted to look up information on Payless' sales strategy. This was not easily done as many of the articles are discussing the collapse of the business vs what made the business operate for so long. I did find a case study by Customer Communications Group (CCG)[26] where Payless, after closing stores and filing for bankruptcy in 2017, attempted to modernize their customer experience. It became clear as I read this report, that the paper was written from a positive point of view because CCG, who wrote the paper, did the work. This

---

[26] https://www.customer.com/retail-marketing/resources/case-studies/payless-delivering-the-case-for-crm/

analysis established that the information Payless was working with in regard to customer data was built on the idea that the consumers visiting Payless doors were willing to utilize loyalty programs or e-mail lists. CCG made a smart decision, but they were too early to help Payless.

There is an uncomfortable conversation that has to take place for Payless and urban accounts operating on price. The conversation has to focus on race and class. Payless stores were located in areas with a high concentration of Black and Brown customers. Payless shoe stores were also located in locations of low- lower middle income neighborhoods that usually sat near or in the same area as Wal-Mart stores or in strip malls. The lease locations of these stores were problematic and required a different approach to consumer relationships.

Black, Brown and low income families deal with upheaval. As someone who grew up in these areas I can tell you that I attended six different schools from first grade to sixth grade. This meant that we moved each year and in many instances our information changed.

This is still the case in these areas today, even with the advent of smart phones and better technology. Low-income families don't have the same access to the internet as middle income families and the level of trust with technology[27] *was* very problematic. CCG was attempting to work with Payless on the premise that low-income households function in the same manner as middle income families. This wasn't the case in 2017, but today things have changed considerably.

Only two years ago the cash customer was still a cash customer who wouldn't trust loyalty programs and didn't offer a chance to capture data for retail.

Those same customers today are utilizing Cash App to transfer money and have their paychecks disbursed to their Cash App cards. While the problem of trust hasn't subsided, today's consumer, for companies attempting to cater to consumers based on price, is more open to rewards programs and therefore more open to becoming a part of the digital ecosystem.

---

[27] https://www.fastcompany.com/3038792/what-i-learned-from-building-an-app-for-low-income-americans

I made an unofficial visit to a Nike Employee Store and a Footlocker. I was visiting both as a customer. I was able to watch returns at each of these stores: as I stood in the lobby waiting to get in to the Nike Store; and as I stood speaking with various employees while I shopped at Foot Locker.

These new entrants into the digital financial arena are still learning how electronic transactions take place. The customers returning products didn't quite understand the policy on how long it took for their money to show up on their cards after the return. As this new/old customer learns how digital transactions work, brands and retailers are using loyalty programs and apps to educate the consumer on how they can shop online and pick up in store. Nike uses its store athletes to enroll visitors into the Nike App. The benefits are Friends and Family discounts and a record of purchases by the visitor to their doors. The customer can also find work-out and fitness information, as well as articles on Nike's products. Foot Locker understands this new opportunity and they have updated their loyalty to program from MVP to FLX which allows a customer to utilize their points within one app for every Foot Locker store which includes: Champs, Foot Locker, Footaction, Kids Foot Locker and Eastbay.

The access of digital finance is allowing the low-income demographic the ability to shop online for the first time. The COVID-19 crisis expedited the learning curve.

The new digital consumer is learning that they can avoid the perceived problems in low-income communities of theft, which is giving these consumers an option that was never there for them only a year ago. A customer can order on Amazon and pick up at Kohl's.

While it isn't exactly research and startups may not be focused solely on the Black and Brown consumer, the video[28] in this footnote shows a YouTube personality explaining how people can avoid check cashing and have their paychecks placed on to their Cash App debit cards. This video was recorded in 2019 and it only scratches the surface of the digital immersion of Black and Brown people into e-commerce. With Venmo, PayPal.me, Apple Pay and other digital wallet apps, low-income families are now a growth area for brands and retailers. Nike understands this and has implemented QR codes on all

---

[28] https://www.youtube.com/watch?v=xygcxoL-E8Y

product hangtags and labels. This QR code when scanned invites the consumer to download Nike or SNKRS app.

Amazon understands that some customers don't have living arrangements conducive to drop offs and they have made it a goal to place pick up locations in stores like Rite Aid[29].

While cash is still king, and men and women who need an emergency pair of flats or dress and casual shoes are still going to be around, startups and reemerging businesses can't rely on previous strategies to capture those cash customers. The customer is savvier and you better believe when they enter the store, even if a shoe costs 19 dollars, that customer is going to browse their smart phone to check on an alternative. The question becomes, "How does a new business engage that consumer while also looking towards adding a more conscious consumer?"

---

[29]https://www.geekwire.com/2019/amazon-expands-counter-store-package-pickup-service-thousands-retail-locations/

138

Chapter

14

Opportunities and a Clean Slate

In an analysis the goal is always to use SWOT- Strengths, Weaknesses, Opportunities and Threats. Throughout this reintroduction I focused on the weaknesses and threats associated with businesses catering to customers based on price solely and businesses who fail to understand the importance of how vendors are no longer product providers. While there are obviously a variety of issues, there are also a number of opportunities that arrive with entering the market tabula rasa.

Any other analyst at this point would deliver a set of data on what has sold well in the last few years for other brands to prove that there are opportunities and strengths in this current market. This data could be broken down by things as simple as color of the product, or as detailed as demographics of who purchased those products.

That data won't accomplish what may be required to enter/reenter the market after bankruptcy and after the COVID-19 crisis. Data does inform, but preparing businesses to find the opportunities that exist in the market happens through experimentation and experience.

Data enhances experience. Experience informs decision making. While the best experience arrives from taking action, the next best teacher is a mentor or shared knowledge. This book is shared knowledge. Much of it may be common sense, but education is about introducing and reinforcing to create muscle memory. It's like a beginning surfer heading to Ocean Beach in San Diego. That surfer can read books, watch YouTube videos and buy clothes from *Outerknown* so they can dress like Kelly Slater; none of this prepares the surfer for the moment when their feet can no longer feel the sand shifting underfoot. Once again, the cliché "experience is the greatest teacher," is true, and while what I'm writing might already be familiar, shared knowledge is an excellent wrench in the entrepreneur's toolbox.

Which is why I am sharing a familiar story for those who know me or read my previous book; I want to reinforce that as grim a picture I've painted that all of the lines aren't connected until I tell you where I see opportunity.

After operating a very successful Amazon Seller Central Marketplace account that was affected by a variety of changes in the back end of Amazon's dashboard and in the market, I correctly predicted the shift to DTC by big brands because I was actually living through the introduction of Brand Registries. Now, anyone paying attention to different businesses could have predicted this. Attention to detail is key in protecting one's self. The problem is I saw what was shaping up, but arrogance and the belief that nothing could happen to me caused inaction.

The contraction of opportunities within the Amazon system charted a clear path to what was taking place in the sneaker industry. No one was writing about the changes which included more brand doors opening and heavy investment in digital platforms and content to bring in the consumer; so there wasn't a playbook for a business to adjust during the shift. I could only ride out the experience and reach the final outcome. As I said, I rode it out not with awareness, but arrogance.

As I rode the wave I didn't bail even when the data showed that my business was collapsing, there was one bomb that delivered me the most valuable rush of knowledge I could ever learn. The requirement by Amazon for all Seller Central Marketplace accounts to align with Amazon's return policy seemed small at the time in 2015, but that one adjustment by Amazon created destruction and opportunity. I would see the destructive side, but I ignored it. I would see the opportunity and I acted on it by changing the way my website operated. I didn't pivot though. I just knew it was smart to begin building traffic to my site, but I still stayed the course selling on Amazon.

Amazon, for consumers, has one of the best return policies in the business. Any customer with Amazon Prime can return items free of charge. As Amazon forced Seller Central Marketplace accounts to implement the same return policy, my account experienced an increase in returns to 30% of sold merchandise. As a small business this broke my business as each return was an average of 10 dollars. Amazon's 15% seller's fees combined with a 30% return total and Amazon's Brand Registry (which placed products behind a "Brand Gate") caused my sales numbers to dwindle from half a million a year to a quarter of a million.

The Returns problem is a major flaw in direct-to-consumer and traditional retail. When I became an Amazon shop it was because I wanted to grow quickly. That was a major mistake. I grew quickly but at my own expense.

As I stayed the course with Amazon and I began experiencing the return issues, I thought that this was only affecting small e-commerce companies like me and other people reselling on Amazon. As I made my daily visits to Foot Locker, City Gear and Hibbett Sports, I realized that as retailers ramped up e-commerce, their returns increased considerably. I still didn't take all of the information and act upon it and by 2016 I was out of business and done selling on Amazon in 2017. I could still return to Amazon with the knowledge that I have of how the platform works, but I haven't as I'll explain in a moment.

I spoke to a technologist at Nike while I was in Portland in 2019 and they explained that Nike is facing a serious problem with returns as they've increased their sales through digital. It's getting to the point that the company will soon have to build facilities to take on returns only.

One of the more interesting situations with Nike is that the returns are beginning to make their way into retail locations. In Nike Employee, Clearance and Factory Stores product is being returned, then resold, that has been worn in some instances

I talked about StockX in the earlier chapters because the company is the only platform where there isn't buyer remorse. "Due to the anonymous nature of our live market, we are unable to offer refunds, exchanges or swaps of any kind - including if you ordered the wrong size. The good news is you can always resell with us if you no longer want your item."³⁰

StockX unlike any selling platform out there, brand, resale, retail, is the only sneaker business where you can't return your purchase. It's an amazing policy, but it's also an opportunity for retail and startups attempting to navigate the landscape and create an experience for buyers. If you look deeply into any business there will be small cracks where a creative person can enter and fill that fissure. In the sneaker industry the cracks are small and very limited.

In the sneaker industry the opportunities lie in doing business better.

Let me deviate: An entrepreneur launching a restaurant has an opportunity to capture a new segment because of the diversity of products available for the plentiful palette of people. A startup creating a record label and performance venue catering to small bands will always have new artists entering the music scene. In some businesses there are an abundance of opportunities.

---

[30] https://help.stockx.com/s/article/Are?language=en_US

I don't see that in the sneaker industry. The business is saturated and the companies who are the giants have the capital to adjust and incorporate your ideas. There is one opportunity. A startup is in that room already and I'll get to that, but what remains in abundance in the sneaker industry is the chance to do things with more care for the consumer and the environment. In my opinion these two things are the most important aspects left to capitalize on.

Chapter

15

Sustainability and Sharing as Opportunity

After being invited to speak at the Footwear Innovation Summit 2019 in Los Angeles, I discovered how little I understood about the importance of sustainability in the sneaker industry. Sneakerheads buy more pairs than the average consumer. While this is good for the bank accounts of brands, it's not good for the planet. The love of sneakers contributes to a heavy carbon footprint. I don't have the means to write here with the depth of knowledge needed to explain the importance of changing the way the industry operates, but I will provide a link[31] where you can begin studying the problem our love of the sneaker industry creates. I guess I shouldn't only say that it is sneaker culture contributing to the massive amounts of sneakers being manufactured. The growth of fast fashion and the desire for cheap

---

[31] https://runrepeat.com/eco-sneakers-research

footwear contributes to the problem of pollution created by kicks as well. There are a range of factors that require their own book to deliver information to be read and shared. (This is an opportunity.)

During the panel discussion at the Footwear Innovation Summit 2019 in Los Angeles a question was asked, "Will the sharing economy work in the footwear and apparel industry?" I initially said that it wouldn't because people simply aren't going to wear someone else's kicks. I boldly responded that people wouldn't participate and that the brands have found a way to continuously push new product to the consumer via subscription boxes and direct-to-consumer methods.

Susan Olivier, VP at Dassault Systems, responded that the sharing economy can and is working. As the event drew to a close it hit me that I answered in haste. It became more apparent that I answered too quickly as my phone began buzzing about a number of different programs that had already launched.

After the summit ended I got a text from Fabian Krauss, Global Business Development Manager at EOS. He hit me with a picture from his hotel room. The picture was of a program New Balance created named "Westin Workout Gear Lending x New Balance". New Balance, a major sneaker company, was already actively participating in the sharing economy by providing The Westin with footwear and apparel for guests to utilize in their workout facilities.

This is an area where brands can improve their carbon footprint. Since this is a book on how businesses can be born of difficult times, creating *Workout Footwear and Apparel Lending Businesses* could be an opportunity for a startup who can work with retail outlets to help clear inventory. Let me get back to the text from Fabian.

When he wrote, he explained, "Yeah, I stayed at the Westin Bonaventure, but heard they also have it at other Westins. I tried it, but they were out of large shirts and shorts. Either a bad sign or a good one since many people do it. The Shoes worked and they looked pretty new…"

When I heard *sharing economy*, my first thought was Uber and Lyft or maybe Plato's Closet. It really never occurred to me that the travel industry and the sneaker industry could be one of the best ways to implement sharing. While many wouldn't consider that traveling light would benefit the world or have anything to do with sustainability, consider that business travel generates these numbers (from US Travel Answer Sheet)[32] you can find leisure travel on this link as well:

- Direct spending on business travel by domestic and international travelers, including expenditures on meetings, events and incentive programs (ME&I), totaled $327.3 billion in 2018.
- ME&I travel accounted for $135.9 billion of all business travel spending.
- U.S. residents logged 463.6 million person-trips* for business purposes in 2018, with 38% for meetings and events.

New Balance locked into an additional revenue stream with Marriott Bonvoy. The opportunity is there for other brands to work with other hotels. But when you consider the decreased weight on flights, the additional miles saved on personal footwear and apparel used, the sharing economy around gear lending is actually a solid option for helping to improve the global carbon footprint. As creative minds begin to look at ways to increase sharing in the footwear and

---

[32] https://www.ustravel.org/answersheet

apparel industry maybe, the constant churning out of products will slow down... probably not, but the industry needs baby steps.

There is additional irony in my rushed answer on the sharing economy. My rush to respond is embarrassing, but it's important that I share how answering in haste, or reacting to business in haste, can deliver poor results. I completely overlooked where I came from in answering too quickly. When I started my first footwear company in 2004, it was funded by my work in reselling shoes. While I would buy shoes from various retail outlets, I would also buy entire collections, clean them up and flip them. My answering too fast also left out the fact that I had already been a consumer in the sharing economy in sneakers. Over twenty years ago in San Diego *RoadRunner Sports* sold slightly used footwear in their showroom. The running shoe business has a high return rate because people don't tend to visit a podiatrist or orthopedic specialist when beginning a workout routine. People will buy what is being marketed and often pick up footwear that doesn't suit their gait, weight or goals. RoadRunner Sports created their own resale opportunities. At the start of my business I did something similar.

In sneaker culture we took to using the words deadstock for new, unworn kicks, and when we had to sell shoes to other people and explain that the shoes had been tried on or gently worn we use the words Nearly Deadstock (NDS) and when they have been worn a few times we use Very Nearly Deadstock (VNDS). When I launched my eBay store I sold a ton of used footwear. Even today I can still buy used or damaged shoes and clean them and make them look like new. The sharing economy has long existed in sneaker culture.

If I want to look back even farther, I have been a part of the sharing economy my entire life. Growing up in a low-income family we shared clothing with friends and family. They were called hand-me-downs. I was *dead wrong* in my response on that panel, but in answering without really going through my mental rolodex I was able to see opportunities.

It's like the Amazon situation where I could see the problems but I didn't respond. In 2019 because of a conference based on improving sustainability in the footwear industry, I learned of options that are informing this book. As I said earlier there aren't many places for businesses to enter the sneaker industry. The chance to create or reenter happens with being better, and as I mentioned *returns* offer a unique opportunity to capitalize on the growth of big brands and to assist smaller brands.

Chapter

16

Limited Opportunities Isn't a Bad Thing

Earlier in the book I listed a group of startup shoe companies. My goal was to show that if someone has a business plan that accounts for the overcrowded, saturated sneaker industry, an entrepreneur, startup group or reemerging company can still break through and create jobs and opportunities. It won't be easy.

As I stated we are in the *'dot com' boom of the 90s* as it relates to the sneaker industry. Companies are gaining investments and new companies pop-up and disappear on a weekly basis. Kickstarter is funding companies giving these crowd funded businesses a head start. This is a good thing, but it's also problematic. The internet has allowed for a more connected society, but it has also democratized the process of beginning a business. In many ways it has removed many of the steps and obstacles, creating business people who haven't had to learn the hard lessons that arrive with the difficult moments of being a business owner.

StockX and GOAT have simplified the e-commerce third party sneaker business. Sellers who might have learned all of the aspects of running a sneaker shop, don't have the bumps in the road which slows a business owner down and gives them the critical lessons needed to withstand slow selling product or problems with warehousing. Today we are in a different time. If time was a house in the summer it would have very small windows and few breezes to cool down the rooms.

In the previous chapter I made the statement that there is really only one clear opportunity. I brought up RoadRunner Sports. RoadRunner Sports was onto something in the 90s. *Return to vendor* was a complicated process that required shipping and receiving costs. When a customer returned a shoe, there weren't a lot of options if that runner had logged miles in the pair. The shoe was still new, but couldn't be resold. When RoadRunner placed their *'pre-owned' sneaker store* within a store in their warehouse, it was ahead of its time.

A startup launched in 2019 in Portland named RESKU, expanded on the concept. RESKU created a partnership with Nike to take on slightly worn product, clean it and resell the product via their website. This allowed Nike to participate in the circular economy and created jobs.

RESKU has one of the best names I've seen in resale. You can read the name as Rescue; rescuing footwear that could end up dumped in a landfill hurting the environment. Or you can read the name as Re-SKU. A SKU is a stock keeping unit. In warehousing all items are given a SKU so it can be tracked. To take a shoe that has been previously worn and to re-sku it is an obvious idea.

RESKU is giving footwear a longer life and adding on to the sustainability movement in a very smart manner. RESKU presents one of the few opportunities which exist in the sneaker industry. Because RESKU only works with Nike, this means brands like New Balance, adidas, Under Armour and a host of other big companies in all of footwear are not currently organized and creating an outlet for the increasing returns they are encountering. Think about the fact that large chains like Foot Locker and JD Sports are also dealing with countless returns and the man-hours associated with audits and RTVs and returns become one of the biggest opportunities for someone looking for a new opportunity in kicks.

Are there other opportunities outside of returns? Yes, of course there are. I was reminded of an option during the writing of this book. The option falls in line with providing better customer service by brands. *Heeluxe* was founded in 2009 by a physical therapist, Dr. Geoffrey A. Gray. The immediate assumption I'm sure is Dr. Gray probably made something that would improve performance aspects of footwear. He did, but it's not in the way that you think.

Heeluxe brought together scientists and therapists to create a process to improve how footwear is tested and designed.

> "Footwear brands asked us to create testing systems that provides fast, easy to understand testing results based on how their customers use the product in the real world. Heeluxe solves this need and goes beyond

expectations by providing recommendations on how to improve your product based on our database of >1,400 tested shoes—eliminating the guesswork and unifying your teams during your design, development, sales, and marketing process.."[33]

It's important that I added Heeluxe because the company was created out of necessity. Heeluxe provides checks and balances in an industry where brands make claims about their product based on their own testing. Remember when Shape Ups, Fit Flops and other footwear claimed to tone your legs simply by walking in their shoes? Remember when a class action lawsuit required those brands that made those claims to pay people who purchased those products and didn't gain the benefits marketed?

A year after the 2008 recession Heeluxe was established. Like today with the COVID-19 crisis causing the economy to stutter, Dr. Geoffrey saw an opportunity to improve the footwear industry. He wasn't someone embedded in the sneaker business. He came from

---

[33] https://www.heeluxe.com/heeluxe-completes-53-shoe-studies-3rd-quarter-2016/

healthcare and therapy to create one of the smartest companies in sportswear.

Consider if you are launching a startup footwear company in the performance space. Unlike Nike and adidas you can't afford to have a research and development department to test the product. Heeluxe allows your small company to factor in the cost of having footwear tested. This will allow you to deliver marketing and materials around your startup to potential customers. In 2009 when I launched ARCH the footwear brand, had I known about Heeluxe, this might be a completely different book.

I know I've stated that there aren't a lot of opportunities remaining in the sneaker industry, but the few that remain offer an abundance of branches to improve upon. Entrepreneurs, startups, small businesses and reemerging companies serving the sneaker industry can:

- develop software
- become marketing gurus
- improve supply chain issues

- work to increase the knowledge and practices around sustainability.

Sure all of these things are already being done, but *everything* can be improved upon and that's why I wrote this book. I put this book together because COVID-19 was the match. The oxygen and fuel was already here. The crisis brought attention to an industry that needs to be improved. As footwear and marketing executive Drew Greer states often, "the industry must D.I.E (Diversification, Inclusiveness and Empowerment)"[34]. The billion dollar sneaker business was disrupted because:

1. Sneakers are produced in an inefficient manner contributing to health issues for those constructing the shoes.
2. The materials utilized are often toxic to both people and the environment.
3. Sneakers are produced in countries around the globe and then exported/imported which is extremely bad for the environment because of the carbon footprint created during manufacturing, shipping and receiving.

---

[34] https://www.linkedin.com/in/drewgreer/

4. Shoes are created with products that in many instances are unable to be upcycled and recycled.

I could continue to add to this list, but the reality is, the moment companies found that they could make shoes cheaper in different countries and import them at a price allowing for incredible markups, they conditioned the sneaker consumer to a market where footwear became disposable.

The reason there are so few 'new' opportunities in the industry is because when people completely lose the need for shoe cobblers, and fast fashion determines what is no longer in style, the culture and the environment is damaged.

After researching companies like COMUNITYmade and discovering that a shoe can be made in the U.S., my eyes were opened to the opportunity and the importance of manufacturing at home.

The U.S. economy is built on consumerism and trade. The moment COVID-19 hit and stopped trade the American economy revealed how fragile it is. This may be a sneaker book, but honestly you can take the word sneaker out and replace it with almost anything sold in the U.S. and the discussion remains the same. *The New Normal* is a wake-up call. The ability to connect with people globally is a beautiful thing; however the global connection is a glass warehouse sitting on a soft first story. All countries have to reinvest in production and job creation on the home front.

This book was supposed to be about the problems with the sneaker industry that allows one person to make a million dollars in 18 months operating in the grey area of sneaker retail. COVID-19 created an opportunity for a different discussion. I hope what you've read here leads you to look at all industries in the U.S. that need to be revamped. I hope that explaining resale provided insight into the holes waiting to be plugged by some creative person. I hope this collection of thoughts makes sense and possibly sparks the next Heeluxe, COMUNITYmade, or NinetyNine.

I hope the book drives a change in how companies born in the United States take on the much needed responsibility of educating consumers; because let's be honest… the Coronavirus isn't what created this new recession. The virus simply expedited the collapse. The rush to cheap consumer goods is at the core of the collapse of the U.S. This country can change only when businesses, sole proprietorships and corporations, begin to care about people and the environment.

Chapter

17

Addendum

Note: *In this section I discuss ASICS, adidas and Nike's foray into investments in small businesses. I did not contact any of these companies. The information utilized in this section is readily available and I've included links to articles in the footnotes. I also spend time building a case study on Foot Locker's investments into Rockets of Awesome and Super Heroic. Neither Rockets of Awesome, nor Super Heroic was involved in the writing of this chapter. My analysis and comparison to Nike's Future Series and Nike Adventure Club is based on my own research.*

This book is becoming a revision of a revision, lol. On 5-14-2020, I submitted the book to prepare for the release on June 1st, 2020 (today is June 2nd, 2020 and I'm still revising, smh). Later that day I realized I left out an extremely important block of information. For those who are creating businesses that work in support of the sneaker industry, I wrote that right now was similar to the investments that took place during the *dot com boom of the 90s*. What I failed to explain was that sneaker brands have begun to create venture capital platforms looking for the next big idea.

I've been writing posts about these investments and I felt that I needed to add this section so that if you're reading this book you can begin to research and possibly find backing for your ideas. I also wanted you to be aware there is still room for your great idea.

ASICS created the **ASICS Venture Corporation**. This corporation has invested in a variety of startups:

> **Seevix Material Sciences Ltd.** ("Seevix"), founded in 2014... Seevix produces patented[1] man-made spidersilk, SVX ™, possessing natural spidersilk's extraordinary strength and elas

ticity. SVX spidersilk is durable, yet sustainable and biodegradable.[35]

Pulse Active Stations Network ("Pulse Active Stations"), a startup that is building a connected network of smart health kiosks across India.[36]

PYRATES Smart Fabrics, a Spanish startup that develops and supplies advanced and responsible fabrics. PYRATES Smart Fabrics was established in 2014.[37]

Curv Labs, Inc., a Canadian startup that developed software to capture motion. A startup that was founded in 2017, Curv Labs has developed software which transforms cameras on mobile devices into a motion capture tool. Using AI vision technology, the software enables smartphones and other mobile devices to measure user motion for analysis.[38]

Aura Vision, a startup that provides in-store analytics for of fline retailers, was founded in 2017 and provides in-store

---

[35] https://corp.asics.com/en/press/article/2020-05-14-3
[36] https://corp.asics.com/en/press/article/2020-03-27-1
[37] https://corp.asics.com/en/press/article/2019-09-26-2
[38] https://corp.asics.com/en/press/article/2019-06-26-1

analytics for offline retailers, using their existing security cameras.[39]

adidas, like ASICS and other brands, has also placed considerable emphasis on investment. Through their **Sports Accelerator**,

> (adidas) selected 13 start-ups that will move parts of their teams to the Station F campus in January. The selected start-ups include "Overtime" – a sports network for the digital generation (US, NY), "Hero" – a live shopping service that connects online shoppers with store associates (UK, London/US, NY) and "Running Care" – a digital coach that helps runners to prevent and treat running injuries (France, Lille) as well as Blue Bite, SneakerCrypt, Storr, WOM, YEAY, eyecandylab, Radius8, Stuffstr, Vekia, and Neurun.[40]

Nike has been acquiring startup companies. As a part of their CDO strategy, they invested into Invertex,[41] Zodiac and Grabbit. I

---

[39] https://corp.asics.com/en/press/article/2019-06-03-2
[40] https://www.adidas-group.com/en/media/news-archive/press-releases/2019/adidas-launches-sports-accelerator-program-platform/
[41] https://arch-usa.com/nike-inc-acquires-invertex-as-a-solution-for-the-home-becoming-the-dressing-room/

mention these investments by the big players in the sneaker industry to establish that there are opportunities in building technology and businesses in support of the business, but the movement is fast and even companies gaining investments can stumble quickly. In my previous book I briefly discussed the new kid's footwear brand *Super Heroic*. FootLocker invested into the kids company and as I said earlier in the book, creating something new is difficult. Bigger companies can quickly disrupt or shift into your lane. Consider how Nike developed a shoe that catered to kids in their *Future Series*, more on that later. After Nike rolled out Future Series they took a platform that was basically dormant, Easykicks.com, and relaunched it in a bigger way after FootLocker's investment into Super Heroic.

Nike had been working with Easykicks since 2017. I honestly didn't know about it, but as I began looking at their 2019 "investment" into Easykicks.com I got a bit of insight that forced me to shift gears. Nike launched the **Nike Adventure Club**, a rebranding of Easykicks and my immediate thought was, "Nike is showing how aggressive they are by disrupting a Footlocker investment that is barely taking off," that was my first thought. What am I talking about here?

Footlocker's investments into *Rockets of Awesome* and *Super Heroic* by the end of 2019 and heading into 2020 were disrupted. Why this happened I'm not sure. Super Heroic shut down this year (2020) and Rockets laid-off half of its staff and closed half of its stores[42].

The investments into Rockets and Super Heroic were extremely smart by FootLocker and I thought they would help to offset the issues involved with relying so heavily on Nike. Now, I can't say with certainty that the launch of Nike Adventure Club disrupted both of FootLocker's young companies, but a natural correlation is that Nike thought that Footlocker's investments were smart as well. They thought it was so smart that they bit the move in taking the effort to rebrand and promote the Nike Adventure Club. The timing is ironic as Nike decided to go public with a full takeover of the concept at back to school time in 2019.

Why am I including this discussion in an extra chapter on opportunities for startups? Reality... As pessimistic as I was in saying there aren't many opportunities, I also know that a lot of investment is tak-

---

[42] https://www.fastcompany.com/90470390/the-trendy-kids-brand-rockets-of-awesome-is-the-latest-dtc-to-stumble

ing place, but it would be unfair for me to discuss the positive without the reality check that bigger brands can always disrupt smaller companies. Let me continue.

While a Nike subscription service can only provide athletic apparel, and Rockets of Awesome could provide a full range of apparel, when Footlocker invested in Super Heroic, who had a very similar concept in getting kids to be more active like Rockets, I saw it as an opportunity to strengthen the Rockets of Awesome platform. I also saw Super Heroic gaining momentum via being placed in Footlocker's doors. The Future Series sneakers created by Nike, in my opinion, disrupted Super Heroics momentum. It appeared to me that Nike kept a careful eye on Super Heroic. Why else would a brand that already had the hearts of kids via athletes, introduce the 2018 Future Series shoe line for kids?

When Nike created the Future Series, I was worried. When Nike launched the Nike Adventure Club, I asked the question, 'Should Footlocker be concerned?'

In my discussion on customers, parents and professionals, I used the Forrest Gump allusion to establish that relationships are at the heart of successful businesses. When I asked if FootLocker needed to be worried I knew the answer was yes because I've said any company relying on big brands to be the backbone of their business places themselves in a difficult position. DTC has pushed brands towards the consumer. COVID-19 forced brands to move even closer to the consumer.

Nike's encroachment into kid's subscription boxes was a venture to capture the internet savvy consumers, not the cash customers transitioning into digital. Those consumers, parents, were more likely to already be a part of Nike's digital ecosystem via apps.

Footlocker, made two solid investments, but it seems they didn't figure out how to integrate the companies seamlessly across the multiple platforms. Neither Rockets of Awesome or Super Heroic in 2019 could be found quickly on Footlocker.com or on GOAT (which makes sense), but if a company is going to invest in multiple companies there should be a team insuring that there is information readily available on every channel, marketing and e-commerce, to make sure that the stories and introductions are being made. The combination of

Rockets and Super Heroic, could have been an important growth area for FootLocker featuring private label as a buffer against Nike's CDO.

What happened instead was Nike launched Nike Adventure Club and the coverage and interest was incredible. At the same time, none of the articles and coverage on business websites mentioned Footlocker's kid's subscription service in comparison. Within a year of FootLocker's investments into two different startups, a big player entered the battle and within a year both of the startups who garnered investments, were broken.

Is this to dishearten you? No, because even within this section there was an opportunity mentioned. In the previous paragraph I said that FootLocker had invested into different startups, but failed to integrate them into their websites and platforms. If you had a team of techs and strategists, you could build a business that assisted companies in streamlining the integration of platforms. There are a variety of situations which can create opportunities.

I could dive into other brands and their investments, but the book has to stop somewhere and what better way to end this than by saying there aren't any dumb or stupid ideas. There are only ideas that haven't been given serious consideration and analysis. Is this industry saturated? Yeah, but almost every industry is crowded. Your job is to find your lane, grade it, pave it, get it on the map and then ride it to where you want to be.

Stay Motivated

www.ingramcontent.com/pod-product-compliance
Lightning Source LLC
Chambersburg PA
CBHW030635220526
45463CB00004B/1536